Flavors of the
GARDENS

 Callaway Gardens

To order additional copies of

Flavors of the Gardens

call 1-800-CALLAWAY (225-5292)

1st Printing   February 2000   10,000

Printed in the USA by

WIMMER

The Wimmer Companies

Memphis

1-800-548-2537

Table of Contents

Introduction

Remove nothing from the Gardens except nourishment for the soul,
consolation for the heart, and inspiration for the mind.

Each year, the volunteers at Callaway Gardens provide a covered-dish picnic at Robin Lake Beach. Lucky Callaway Gardens staff members that work with the volunteers throughout the year are invited to the picnic as a gesture of the volunteers' appreciation. Now, this may seem somewhat backwards, because it's the faithful corps of more than 600 volunteers who helps the staff in a million ways; however, the volunteers want to express their thanks for the friendly environment that the Gardens' employees provide. And the staff loves this picnic!

The fare at this picnic is extraordinarily delicious, and we never get far beyond the first bites when the requests for recipes begin. Before it's all over, someone always suggests that these recipes would make a wonderful cookbook. Everyone enthusiastically agreed, of course, but for years it never got further than a suggestion.

Finally, in 1997, a cookbook committee was formed, and recipes were solicited from Gardens' employees and volunteers. The recipes poured in and, as the saying goes, the rest is history.

This cookbook was designed to incorporate the beauty and flavor of Callaway Gardens with wonderful Southern recipes. Just as the food is a feast for one's palate, Callaway Gardens is a feast for one's eyes and spirit.

The Callaway Gardens volunteers give time and energy to the Gardens in exchange for being part of a place of peace; having the companionship of people who share a love for the Gardens; and the pleasure of helping visitors enjoy the beauty and serenity that is here. We hope that we are able to share some of that beauty and serenity with you through the pages of this book.

Foreword

Cason Jewell Callaway, co-founder of Callaway Gardens, was born in LaGrange, Georgia, as the son of Fuller Earle and Ida Cason Callaway. Cason's father was a self-made success in the business world, and by the year of Cason's birth in 1894, Fuller Callaway had built a strong retail business in LaGrange and was just a few years short of running his first mill.

By the way people treated him, Cason quickly learned that he was the son of an important man. However, his father told him not to get "puffed up." His social standing only meant he would have to work twice as hard as anyone else. Fuller did not like the idea that his success would keep Cason from knowing the adversity that builds character.

Fuller need not have worried, for Cason grew into a hard working young man with a good business acumen and the ability to visualize beauty where others saw nothing. Cason received his education and served in the Navy. Shortly after he returned from the Navy, he met a young woman, Virginia Hand, at a party in Atlanta. He knew this was the woman he would marry. Cason and Virginia wed in her hometown of Pelham, Georgia, on April 3, 1920.

Cason and Virginia lived in LaGrange where Cason's career in textiles followed his father's footsteps. He had a knack for success and did well in the industry.

During the Depression, Cason's thoughts turned from textiles to his family retreat at Blue Springs, south of LaGrange. Blue Springs, named after the brilliant blue water that flowed from natural springs in the area, was where the Callaway family enjoyed a cottage, private lake, spring-fed pool, a pavilion for entertaining, and horses. He and Virginia hosted many friends and dignitaries including neighbor Franklin D. Roosevelt who frequented the area for polio treatment.

Cason's projects at Blue Springs gave him freedom and a refreshing change. Finally, in 1935 Cason decided to leave the mills. He named his brother, Fuller Jr., president, and by 1938 he retired completely from the cotton industry.

With his attention focused on Blue Springs, Cason began farming wholeheartedly, experimenting with various crops and animals and learning how to make the tired land come alive through crop rotation, terracing and fertilization. He developed the Better Farms Program that was an innovative partnership between businesses and farmers, providing farmers with the means to learn how to productively work their land. This successful program gained national attention as almost all of the farms in the program showed a profit.

On a walk through the woods one day, Cason discovered a small shrub covered with brilliant orangish-red blooms. He didn't readily recognize the plant so he took a branch to Virginia, who was a horticulturist at heart. After some investigation, Virginia discovered that the plant was the prunifolia azalea. This rare plant grew naturally only within a 100-mile radius of Blue Springs. Its beauty and rarity compelled the Callaways to set aside their land for the protection of the prunifolia azalea and other native plants.

Their first thoughts were to build a retreat for their friends, where they could relax, enjoy beautiful scenery, play a round of golf and enjoy the company of others. This first vision of Callaway Gardens changed, however, as they saw the land begin to take shape. It seemed far too beautiful for just a few people to see, so they decided to share it with the public.

On May 21, 1952, Callaway Gardens opened its gates. Since then, there have been many changes and additions, and millions of men, women and children have enjoyed all the Gardens has to offer. Today, the Gardens features a full array of recreational activities, luxurious accommodations, restaurants, shops, a calendar full of special events, workshops, symposia and more, all which support the Gardens' purpose to provide a wholesome family environment where all may find beauty, relaxation, inspiration and a better understanding of the living world.

Acknowledgments

A tremendous thank you and a pat on the back goes to every member of the Cookbook Committee for their vision, hours of hard work and undying sense of humor. As with any successful group project, someone must take the lead and provide inspiration and encouragement to others through his or her dedication, perseverance and attitude. That person was Charla Cannon, Chair of the Cookbook Committee, who literally made all the pieces fit together. Not only did she type every letter of every recipe, but she kept each committee member on their assigned task, firmly, yet lovingly. Whenever enthusiasm waned, Charla was there with a smile and word of encouragement. To Charla, our heartfelt thanks for an excellent job!

Cookbook Committee

Charla Cannon, chair

Judy Banks

Janice Boyd

Annie Kate Chambless

Sara Drummond

Amy McGreevy

Beth Rasnick

Suzanne Adams

Shirley Baker

Fran Cadenhead

Kenneth Cadenhead

Lynn Manley

Ernestine McCurdy

Peggy Terry

Appetizers and Beverages

The Herb Garden at Callaway Gardens

A pinch of this and a touch of that...

...can make all the difference in the world when you're cooking. Whether you pronounce it with the "h" or without, herbs are fascinatingly versatile. Not only do they add zest to meals, they also soothe, heal and perfume.

The large Herb Garden in Mr. Cason's Vegetable Garden is filled with a delightful variety of herbs, some of which are used in the restaurants at Callaway Gardens. A weekend each year is devoted to teaching how to incorporate herbs into our daily lives. This herbal weekend includes meals prepared using herbs, tours of the herb garden, and workshops on various uses of these fun and intriguing plants.

A visit to the Herb Garden encourages gardeners to try their hand at their own herb garden. A window garden, container garden or full-fledged herb garden all promise delightful results and turn many gardeners into cooks!

❧ *Bernice's Roasted Pecans*

2	tablespoons margarine		Salt to taste
1	tablespoon vinegar	1	dash cayenne pepper or
2	cups pecan halves		½ teaspoon for hotter nuts

Preheat oven to 400 degrees. Melt butter in iron skillet. Add vinegar and then the pecans. Stir well. Add salt and cayenne pepper. Put into preheated 400 degree oven. Turn oven off and allow to cool. You may leave the pecans in the oven overnight.

This recipe works well because you will not burn the pecans using this method. Recipe may be doubled.

Yield: 2 cups

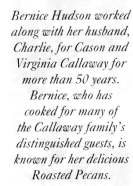

Bernice Hudson worked along with her husband, Charlie, for Cason and Virginia Callaway for more than 50 years. Bernice, who has cooked for many of the Callaway family's distinguished guests, is known for her delicious Roasted Pecans.

Glazed Peanuts

1	egg white, slightly beaten	¼	teaspoon ground cloves
½	cup sugar	4	cups unsalted peanuts
½	teaspoon cinnamon		(1 pound)
½	teaspoon nutmeg		

In a large mixing bowl, combine all ingredients. Stir to coat nuts. Spread on greased cookie sheet. Bake at 250 degrees for 1 hour. Cool. Store in airtight containers.

Yield: 4 cups

Candied Pecans

2	cups pecans	½	teaspoon nutmeg
1	teaspoon vanilla	1½	cups sugar
½	teaspoon salt	½	cup water
1½	teaspoons cinnamon		

Mix all ingredients in sauce pan and cook on top of the stove until soft stage is reached. Turn onto a cookie sheet. When cool (15 to 20 minutes), break into pieces.

Yield: 2 cups

Spiced Pecans

½ cup butter	½ teaspoon cinnamon
2 tablespoons Worcestershire sauce	Dash garlic powder
	Dash ground cloves
1 teaspoon hot pepper sauce	2 cups pecans
½ teaspoon salt	

Place butter in a 2 quart microwave safe dish. Microwave 45 seconds to 1½ minutes or until butter has melted. Mix in Worcestershire sauce, hot pepper sauce, salt, cinnamon, garlic powder and cloves. Stir pecans into mixture. Blend thoroughly. Microwave uncovered 6 to 8 minutes, stirring after 3 minutes. When heated through, spread nuts on paper towel to cool. When cool, place in jars. Screw on lids and store at room temperature.

Yield: 2 cups

"When I stroll around the Gardens and see thousands of people on the beach and in the water, and on the golf course and fishing in the lakes, or just strolling in the woods listening to the birds sing, or looking at the flowers, it makes me feel a fine warm glow of selfish happiness."
— Cason J. Callaway

Curry Dip

1 cup mayonnaise	1 tablespoon Worcestershire sauce
3 tablespoons catsup	
3 teaspoons curry powder	1 medium onion, grated
	¼ teaspoon garlic salt

Mix all ingredients well. Refrigerate.

Yield: 1½ cups

Aloha Fruit Dip

12 macaroons, crushed	1 pint dairy sour cream
¼ cup light brown sugar, firmly packed	1 large pineapple
	Assorted fruits of your choice

Crush macaroons into small pieces. Mix together with sugar and sour cream. Chill several hours to soften the macaroon crumbs. Do not stir again. Core pineapple, removing pineapple pieces for dipping. Fill pineapple shell with fruit dip. Arrange on a platter surrounded by pineapple chunks and slices of assorted fruit.

Yield: 24 servings

Vidalia Onion Dip

1 cup coarsely chopped Vidalia® onion	Paprika
1 cup mayonnaise	Corn chips, tortilla chips or crackers
1 cup grated sharp cheddar cheese	

Combine onion, mayonnaise and cheese. Pour into a 1 quart baking dish. Sprinkle with paprika and bake uncovered in a preheated oven at 350 degrees for 25 minutes. Serve with corn chips, tortilla chips, or crackers.

Yield: 2 cups

Spinach Dip

1 (10 ounce) box frozen chopped spinach, thawed and drained	1 cup mayonnaise
	1 cup sour cream
1 package vegetable soup mix	1 medium onion, chopped

Mix all ingredients and refrigerate at least 24 hours. Serve with crackers.

Yield: 4 cups

Baked Artichoke Dip

1 (14 ounce) can artichoke hearts, chopped	1-2 cloves minced garlic, to taste
¾ cup mayonnaise	¼ teaspoon Worcestershire sauce
1 cup grated Parmesan cheese	
½ cup grated mozzarella cheese (optional)	2 drops hot pepper sauce Melba toast

Combine all ingredients. Spoon into lightly greased 1 quart casserole. Bake at 350 degrees for 20 minutes or until bubbly. Serve with melba toast rounds.

Yield: 2 cups

"What I'm trying to do here is hang the picture a little higher on the wall for the people of this region. Every child ought to see something beautiful before he's six years old — something he will remember all this life."
— Cason J. Callaway

Cranberry and Cilantro Salsa and Brie

½ pound fresh cranberries
½ bunch cilantro
1 clove fresh garlic
¼ cup sugar

Juice of 1 or 2 limes
½-1 teaspoon ginger
Brie cheese
Crackers

Chop cranberries, cilantro and garlic. Mix together with sugar, juice and ginger. Heat cheese, or bring to room temperature. Pour cranberry mixture over and around cheese. Serve with crackers of your choice.

Yield: 16 servings

Shrimp Spread

1 (8 ounce) package cream cheese
⅓ cup mayonnaise
1 teaspoon lemon juice
½ teaspoon minced onion

½ teaspoon Worcestershire sauce
2 tablespoons dry white wine
1 can shrimp, drained and chopped

Combine all ingredients except shrimp. Beat well with electric mixer or by hand. Stir in shrimp last. Serve on crackers or toast cutouts.

Yield: 16 servings

Cheese Biscuits

½ pound sharp cheddar cheese, grated
1 stick butter
1 teaspoon salt

½ teaspoon cayenne pepper
1 cup flour
Pecan halves

Grate cheese and add to creamed butter. Mix well. Then add salt, pepper and flour. Roll into small balls. Place on ungreased cookie sheet and press a pecan half on each ball to flatten out. Bake at 350 degrees for 15 minutes.

Yield: 40 to 50 biscuits

Cream Cheese Beef Ball

4	(2½ ounce) packages luncheon beef slices, diced	3	tablespoons Worcestershire sauce
1	medium onion, grated	2	tablespoons monosodium glutamate (optional)
3	(8 ounce) packages cream cheese, softened		Hot pepper sauce to taste
			Salt and pepper to taste

Add diced beef (reserve enough in which to roll ball) and grated onion to cream cheese. Add remaining ingredients. Mix well, shape into ball, roll in reserved diced beef. May be divided into two or three smaller balls. Keep in refrigerator.

Yield: 24 servings

One of Cason Callaway's closest personal friends was President Franklin D. Roosevelt. Cason said that the two "disagreed fundamentally on all the fundamentals," but they remained close friends.

Pizza Cracker Spread

1	(12 ounce) package cream cheese	2	tablespoons mayonnaise
2	tablespoons minced onion	½	teaspoon garlic powder
1	tablespoon Worcestershire sauce	1	(12 ounce) bottle chili sauce, drained
1	tablespoon lemon juice	8	ounces crabmeat
			Chopped parsley

Blend onion, Worcestershire sauce, lemon juice, mayonnaise and garlic powder into the cream cheese. Spread this mixture flat (like a pizza) on a round tray or plate. Cover with the drained chili sauce. Flake crab over the top of sauce and sprinkle with chopped parsley. Serve with crackers.

Yield: 20 servings

Georgia Crackers

½	cup mayonnaise	1	tablespoon onion flakes, or
½	cup Parmesan cheese		one small grated onion
		24	saltine crackers

Mix mayonnaise, Parmesan cheese and onion. Mound by teaspoon on saltines. Broil until brown. Serve at once.

If one keeps on hand a jar of mayonnaise, a shaker of Parmesan cheese, a jar of onion flakes, and a box of saltines, there is always this good, quick snack to serve with drinks.

Yield: 20 to 24 servings

Tiny Cheese Biscuits

1½	cups all-purpose flour	½	cup butter or margarine,
1	cup shredded sharp		softened
	cheddar cheese	1	large egg, beaten
½	teaspoon ground red pepper	¼	teaspoon water

Combine flour, cheese, and red pepper, mixing well. Cut in butter until mixture resembles coarse crumbs. Add egg and water. Mix well with hands. Shape into 1 inch balls. Place on greased baking sheet. Bake at 400 degrees for 15 minutes.

Yield: 2½ dozen

Cheese Straws

1	stick butter	½	teaspoon cayenne pepper
1½	cups flour	¼	teaspoon garlic powder
1½	teaspoons baking powder	2	cups grated extra sharp
1	teaspoon salt		cheddar cheese

Soften butter (do not melt). Mix with dry ingredients, then add cheese. It is easier to mix with your hands. Place mixture in cookie press using desired disk and press onto ungreased cookie sheet. Bake 10 to 12 minutes at 350 degrees or until golden. Store in air tight container.

Keep in freezer for emergencies — if you can resist eating them.

Yield: 30 servings

Sue Duncan's Cheese-Date Biscuits

½ pound sharp cheddar
  cheese, grated
½ pound butter or margarine
2½ cups flour
½ teaspoon red pepper

½ teaspoon paprika
1 teaspoon salt
1 (10 ounce) package whole
  dates, pitted

Cream butter and cheese. Add other ingredients (except dates) to make a dough. Pinch off enough dough to wrap around each date leaving the dough a bit loose as the dates expand while baking. Bake on ungreased cookie sheet at 350 degrees for 15 to 20 minutes.

Sue suggests not letting them get too brown.

Yield: 20 servings

Cason Callaway designed the first golf course at the Gardens so that the golfer who made the mistake of lifting his head on a shot would see woodland flowers and magnolias. He thought this would allow him to soothe his spirit without cussing.

Snow Peas Stuffed with Crabmeat

½ pound snow peas
4 tablespoons mayonnaise
1 tablespoon lemon juice
3 dashes red pepper sauce

1 teaspoon capers
12 ounces crabmeat
2 hard-boiled eggs, finely
  chopped

Wash and trim peas. Split on top side. Blanch in lightly salted boiling water 10 seconds and submerge in cold water a moment. Drain. Cool. Combine all other ingredients. Stir gently, being careful not to break up crabmeat. Stuff each snow pea with heaping teaspoon of filling. Refrigerate up to 6 hours. Peas can be prepared the day before and refrigerated, covered.

Yield: about 60

Marinated Shrimp Wrapped in Pea Pods

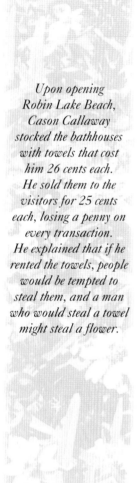

| 2½ | pounds medium shrimp | 1 | pound snow peas, blanched 30 seconds |

Marinade:

¼	cup fresh parsley	2	tablespoons chopped rosemary
1½	cups olive oil		
¼	cup sherry vinegar	½	teaspoon sugar
1½	tablespoons Dijon mustard		Fresh ground pepper, to taste
1	tablespoon fresh lemon juice		
2	teaspoons salt	1	clove garlic, crushed
		2	tablespoons chopped shallots

Cook, peel and devein shrimp. Mix marinade. While shrimp are warm, add marinade. Refrigerate 6 hours or overnight. Split blanched pea pods in half. Wrap a snow pea half around shrimp horizontally and secure with a toothpick. Refrigerate until ready to serve.

Serve on long skewers inserted into pineapple half.

Yield: 50 servings

Upon opening Robin Lake Beach, Cason Callaway stocked the bathhouses with towels that cost him 26 cents each. He sold them to the visitors for 25 cents each, losing a penny on every transaction. He explained that if he rented the towels, people would be tempted to steal them, and a man who would steal a towel might steal a flower.

Scotch Eggs

9	large eggs	1	cup plain bread crumbs
¼	cup all-purpose flour		Oil for deep frying
1	pound mild sausage		

Hard boil 8 eggs. Cool, remove shells, rinse and pat dry. Roll eggs in flour to coat well. Divide sausage in 8 equal portions and pat out to a flat circle. Mold one piece of sausage around each egg. Sausage should cover evenly and have no holes. Beat additional egg in a shallow bowl. Roll each sausage covered egg in beaten egg, then roll each in bread crumbs to coat well. Deep fry each egg in pre-heated oil, browning evenly. Cooking too fast will result in sausage not being cooked through. Drain on paper towel, cool and slice in half.

Scotch eggs are usually eaten cold, by themselves, or with a salad. May be served fresh and hot with a spicy tomato or horseradish sauce. A favorite at the annual Volunteer Picnic!

Yield: 16 servings

Stuffed Cream Puffs

Cream Puffs

½ cup margarine
1 cup water
1 cup all-purpose flour, sifted

½ teaspoon salt
4 large eggs

In a saucepan, combine margarine and water. Bring to a vigorous boil. Reduce heat to low, add flour and salt, which has been sifted together. Stir vigorously until mixture leaves sides of pan and forms a stiff ball. Remove from heat. Add eggs, one at a time, beating hard after each addition. Using either a cookie press with a cream puff tip, or a teaspoon, form cream puffs ½ inch in diameter. Place 1½ inches apart on greased cookie sheet. Bake at 450 degrees for 15 minutes, then 325 degrees for 20 minutes. Remove to cooling racks. When puffs are cool, cut a hole in the side of each. Fill with favorite filling or put in air tight container in cool place to fill later. Can be frozen.

Chicken Salad Stuffing

4 cups cooked and finely chopped chicken
6 large eggs, boiled and mashed fine
½ cup chopped sweet pickles or salad relish
½ cup finely chopped celery

½ cup finely chopped red pimentos
¼ cup almonds, toasted and finely chopped (optional)
Salt to taste
Mayonnaise, as needed

*"You can put a
10 cent flower
in a 50 cent hole
and it will live
and grow and thrive.
But if you put a
50 cent flower
in a 10 cent hole,
it will die."
— Cason J. Callaway*

Mix all ingredients and add mayonnaise to spreading consistency. Stuff cream puffs or make sandwiches.

Shrimp Stuffing

1 pound frozen salad shrimp, cooked or 3 (5 ounce) cans shrimp
1 (8 ounce) package cream cheese
3 large eggs, hard-boiled and mashed fine

2 dashes Worcestershire sauce
½ cup finely chopped celery
1 teaspoon grated onion
¼ teaspoon dry mustard
1 sprinkle black pepper
Mayonnaise as needed

Blend all ingredients and add mayonnaise until spreading consistency. Stuff into cream puffs.

Yield: 30 servings

Zucchini Squares

½	cup canola oil	½	cup grated mozzarella cheese
4	eggs, slightly beaten		
½	teaspoon Bouquet Garni	½	cup grated Parmesan cheese
½	teaspoon seasoned salt	½	cup chopped onion
½	teaspoon salt	1	cup biscuit baking mix
	Dash pepper	3	cups thinly sliced zucchini

Mix in order given. Pour into 9x13 inch pan that has been sprayed with no-stick cooking spray. Bake 25 minutes at 350 degrees. Cut into squares and serve. Freezes well.

Yield: 70 servings

Virginia Callaway once told her husband Cason that she would like a magnolia tree like those that grew at her childhood home in south Georgia. With his usual generosity in meeting her requests, he gave her 5,000 tiny magnolia trees. Many of these trees tower majestically at Callaway Gardens and the local area today.

Salmon Dill Canapés

1	8 ounce fresh salmon steak 1 inch thick		Lettuce leaves
		1	(3½ ounce) jar capers
1	(8 ounce) package light cream cheese	1	small red onion, finely chopped
3	tablespoons fresh dill, or 1 tablespoon dried dill	1	large cucumber, cut into ¼ inch slices
2	tablespoons lemon juice	1	loaf French baguette, thinly sliced
¼	teaspoon salt		
¼	teaspoon pepper		

Place the salmon steak on an unheated rack of a broiler pan. Broil 4 inches from heat for 5 to 7 minutes or until easily flaked with a fork. Cover and chill until needed. Remove skin and bones from salmon. Place salmon in a food processor. Add cream cheese, dill, lemon juice, salt and pepper. Cover and process until smooth. Cover and chill up to 24 hours before serving. To serve, line a large platter with lettuce. Mound the salmon spread in the center. Arrange the capers and onions next to the salmon spread. Fill the rest of the platter with cucumber and bread slices. To assemble canapés, spread cucumber or bread slices with salmon spread and top with capers and onions.

White onion may be used in place of red.

Yield: 40 servings

Pot Stickers

3	cups shredded cabbage	1	tablespoon dry sherry
¾	pound ground pork	1½	teaspoons minced ginger
1	tablespoon chopped green onion	¼	tablespoon monosodium glutamate, optional
3	tablespoons soy sauce		Wonton wrappers

Dipping Sauce

2	tablespoons minced ginger	¼	cup white wine vinegar
¼	cup soy sauce		

Mix first seven ingredients together. Stuff wonton wrappers. Cook in electric skillet on medium high heat for 2 minutes. Reduce heat to low. Gradually add ⅓ cup water. Cover and cook 10 minutes or until done. Serve with dipping sauce.

Yield: 72 servings

Quiche Lorraine L'Escoffier

¼	pound slab bacon, cut in ¼ inch dice	5	eggs
1	(9 inch) pie crust, unbaked	2	cups whipping cream
½	pound Gruyère cheese, grated	¼	teaspoon salt
			Freshly ground pepper
			Pinch freshly grated nutmeg

Preheat oven to 300 degrees. Cook bacon until crisp, drain. Sprinkle bacon over pie shell and top with cheese. Combine eggs and cream in medium bowl and whisk until well blended. Mix in seasonings. Pour over cheese. Bake until quiche is lightly browned, about 1 hour. Cut into wedges and serve.

Excellent for brunch.

Served as an appetizer in the L'Escoffier Room of the Beverly Hilton, Beverly Hills, California, in 1965.

Yield: 6 servings

Cason Callaway enjoyed walking about the Gardens on the weekends, talking with the visitors. Wearing an old Panama hat and a sports shirt, and smoking a long-stemmed church-warden pipe, he'd stop at picnic tables and chat with the people about their work, their children, and what they thought of the Gardens.

Shrimp Toast

½ pound shrimp, peeled and finely chopped
3 strips bacon, finely chopped
5 water chestnuts, finely chopped
1 tablespoon finely chopped green onion
1 tablespoon cooking wine
1½ teaspoons salt
½ teaspoon sugar
¼ teaspoon pepper
¼ teaspoon monosodium glutamate (optional)
4 medium eggs
2 tablespoons cornstarch
14 slices white bread
3 cups cooking oil

Mix shrimp, bacon, water chestnuts and green onion in a bowl. Add wine, salt, sugar, pepper and monosodium glutamate and mix well. Add eggs and cornstarch and mix thoroughly. Remove the crust from sliced bread and cut each slice into 2 triangles. Put about 2½ teaspoons shrimp paste on each slice of bread and spread evenly to edges. Pour oil into large skillet. Heat oil to medium high (350 degrees). Place bread with shrimp side down and cook until edges are brown. Turn and cook other side. Drain and serve.

Yield: 8 servings

Shrimp Rémoulade

2 pounds shrimp
Seafood seasoning of your choice
½ cup minced fresh onion
1½ cups mayonnaise
½ cup mustard, Creole style
¼ teaspoon garlic salt
¼ teaspoon sugar
1 teaspoon horseradish
½ teaspoon celery seed
2 tablespoons Worcestershire sauce
2 tablespoons fresh lemon juice
2 tablespoons capers
Lettuce
Salt and pepper to taste
1 lemon, sliced
Parsley

Boil shrimp 3 to 4 minutes in water and seafood seasoning of choice. Chill. Mince onion in food processor. Blend together ingredients with the exception of shrimp, lettuce, capers, lemon and parsley. Refrigerate 8 hours or overnight. Arrange shrimp on lettuce leaves. Top with sauce followed by a sprinkle of capers. Garnish with lemon slices and parsley.

Sauce left over becomes better the next day. This is a great sauce for broiled or baked fish such as orange roughy or red snapper. Serve instead of tartar sauce.

Yield: 4 servings

The Ida Cason Callaway Memorial Chapel was designed by Cason Callaway to be so much a part of its surroundings that it looked like it grew there. This Gothic-style chapel was a tribute to his mother and a labor of love for Cason. He painstakingly planned every detail of the chapel for ten years, finding the perfect setting, commissioning the stained glass windows, working closely with the architects. He never saw it completed however, because he died less than a week after the plans were completed.

Perky Punch

1 quart water	⅔ cup brown sugar, firmly packed
2 quarts cranberry juice	1 tablespoon whole allspice
2 quarts unsweetened pineapple juice	1 tablespoon whole cloves
Juice of 2 lemons	4 (2 inch) sticks cinnamon

Put juices and water in 30 cup percolator. In basket of percolator, place brown sugar, allspice, cloves, and cinnamon sticks. Perk until done. If mixture thickens, just add water.

Yield: 25 servings

Hot Cider

1 gallon cider	4 sticks cinnamon
½ cup brown sugar	12 whole allspice
¼ teaspoon nutmeg	12 whole cloves

Heat cider and sugar together. Tie spices into a cheese cloth. Add spice bag to cider and simmer for 30 minutes. Do not boil.

Yield: 25 servings

Wassail

1 gallon apple cider or juice	1 cup brown sugar
1 (6 ounce) can frozen lemonade	2 cups water
2 whole cloves	4 sticks cinnamon

Mix all ingredients together. Heat and serve. Works well in crockpot or percolator.

Yield: 22 servings

The Masters Water-ski Tournament, an international competition featuring the world's greatest water skiers, is a Memorial Day weekend tradition at Robin Lake Beach. This event marks the beginning of Summer at Callaway Gardens.

Russian Tea

1	gallon water, divided	5	tablespoons tea leaves
1	tablespoon whole cloves	1	(14 ounce) can pineapple
1	tablespoon allspice		juice
2	sticks cinnamon	1	(14 ounce) can orange juice
4½-6	cups sugar	1	(8 ounce) can grapefruit juice

Combine cloves, allspice and cinnamon in ½ gallon water and let boil slowly 10 minutes. Strain, pour over sugar while hot. Pour this mixture, while still hot, over tea leaves and let steep for 5 minutes. Strain again, then add ½ gallon cold water. Mix juices together and add the gallon of spiced tea. Serve hot or cold.

Yield: 2 gallons

Ice Rings for Punch

1	(6 ounce) can frozen orange juice concentrate	Red or green grapes
1	(6 ounce) can frozen lemonade	Lemon or orange slices

Mix orange juice and lemonade with water according to directions. Fill ice ring mold ⅓ full of juices. Freeze until firm, but not solid. Place washed fruit in desired arrangement. (Remember the ring will be inverted when used). Slowly fill with juice without disturbing the fruit. If the fruit begins to float, press down into the frozen section. Return to freezer until secure. Fill with remaining juice and freeze until solid. When ready to use, unmold gently and float in the punch. As the ring melts, it will not dilute the punch.

Berries, cherries, etc. and fresh mint leaves may be used in place of grapes and citrus fruits with your favorite punch recipe.

Yield: 1 ice ring

Georgia Peach Celebration Starter

4 cups peaches, ripe and peeled	Juice and grated rind of 1 orange
⅓ cup sugar	2 cups cold champagne
¼ cup Grand Marnier	Twisted orange strips

Purée peaches and sugar in blender. Add Grand Marnier, juice and grated rind. Keep chilled. When ready to serve, slowly stir in champagne. Spoon into crystal stemware. Garnish with orange strips. Enjoy.

Yield: 4 servings

Peaches are easiest peeled by submerging the fruit in boiling water for 20 to 30 seconds, then immediately transferring to a bowl of ice water. The skin should slip off easily with the help of a paring knife.

Citric Acid Punch

1 quart cold water	⅓ cup lemon juice, chilled
1 ounce citric acid	3 quarts clear carbonated drink, chilled
4 pounds sugar	
1 (46 ounce) can pineapple juice, chilled	

Bring the water to a boil. Add citric acid and sugar. Stir until dissolved. Let stand overnight at room temperature in a plastic or glass container. Immediately before serving, add the chilled juices and chilled carbonated drink. Mix. Makes a pretty yellow punch but can be changed by the addition of food coloring.

Despite the name, this is a very refreshing beverage. Citric acid is available in the canning section of grocery stores.

Yield: 50 servings

Gin is flavored with dry juniper berries.

Sloe Gin Daiquiri

Crushed ice
1 (6 ounce) can frozen pink lemonade
4 ounces rum
4 ounces sloe gin
2 tablespoons sugar
Cherries, as needed

Fill blender with crushed ice. Add ingredients and blend until frosty. Serve in cocktail glasses with a cherry.

Yield: 6 servings

Mint Julep

12 sprigs fresh mint
6 lumps sugar
12 jiggers bourbon
Crushed ice as needed

Use a twelve or sixteen ounce silver goblet or tall glass for each individual drink. Crush a sprig of mint against each goblet or glass, discard mint. Dissolve a lump of sugar in a tablespoon of water in each glass. Fill each glass or goblet half full of crushed ice. Add two jiggers of bourbon and stir gently. Garnish with sprig of fresh mint.

Yield: 6 servings

Strawberry Daiquiri

Crushed ice, as needed
1 (6 ounce) can frozen lemonade
4 ounces frozen strawberries
6 ounces rum
3 tablespoons strawberry flavored brandy

Fill blender with crushed ice, add frozen lemonade, frozen strawberries, rum and strawberry flavored brandy. Blend until frosty and serve in cocktail glasses.

Yield: 6 servings

Banana Daiquiri

	Crushed ice	1	fresh banana
1	(6 ounce) can frozen	2	ounces banana flavored
	lemonade		brandy
6	ounces rum		

Fill blender with crushed ice and add ingredients. Blend until frosty and serve in cocktail glasses.

Yield: 6 servings

Eggnog

12	eggs, separated	2	quarts whole milk
1½	cups bourbon	1	quart whipping cream
¾	cup sugar		Nutmeg as needed

Beat egg yolks until lemon colored. Add bourbon slowly, a jigger at a time. Add sugar slowly, add milk and beat well. Cover bowl and refrigerator over night. Just before serving, beat egg whites until stiff, fold into yolk-milk mixture. Beat cream until stiff and add nutmeg. Pour over mixture. Ladle into cups so that each cup is topped with a layer of whipped cream and nutmeg.

Yield: 30 servings

Hirko Cooler

1	(12-16 ounce) can frozen	1	(33.8 ounce) bottle piña
	orange juice		colada mix
1	(36 ounce) bottle orange	2	cups vodka
	juice		Lemon-lime soda

Mix all ingredients. Pour into large container and put into freezer to form a "slush" type mixture. Pour into a glass of lemon-lime soda and stir. The vodka can be increased to taste or add more soft drink. This will remain in the freezer as long as desired or until the family or relatives find out it is there.

Yield: 15 servings

Cason and Virginia Callaway first visited Blue Springs in 1921 on a picnic with friends. The area intrigued them and they became frequent visitors, exploring the woodlands around the crystal blue pool and eventually purchasing 2,500 acres.

Frozen Alexander

½   gallon vanilla ice cream   1   cup crème de cacao
½   cup brandy

Soften ice cream slightly and cut into chunks. Place into large mixing bowl. Add liquors. Mix on slow speed of mixer until smooth. Serve in brandy snifters.

Yield: 8 servings

During a hike one summer, Cason discovered a shrub with reddish-orange blossoms. He showed a branch to Virginia who identified it as Rhododendron prunifolium, or plumleaf azalea. This rare plant was native only to the area around Pine Mountain and blooms in the natural woodlands in July and August. The flower of this plant is incorporated into the Callaway Gardens logo.

Syllabub

2   cups white wine or sherry   Heavy cream, whipped
½   cup granulated sugar   Granulated sugar
½   teaspoon ground nutmeg   Cinnamon
2   quarts cold milk

In a serving bowl, blend wine with sugar and nutmeg. Place milk in blender, 2 cups at a time, and mix until frothy. Pour into bowl. Stir and serve in punch cups. Top each serving with whipped cream which has been seasoned by slowly adding 1 tablespoon sugar and 1 teaspoon cinnamon.

Yield: 20 (4 ounce) servings

Keeokee Coffee

1   cup brewed coffee   ½   jigger brandy
½   jigger Kahlúa liqueur   Whipped cream

Combine coffee, Kahlúa and brandy. Top with whipped cream. Serve hot.

Yield: 1 serving

Breads

The Ida Cason Callaway Memorial Chapel

Deep in the heart of Callaway Gardens...

...lies one of the most beautiful tributes a son has ever made to his mother. The Ida Cason Callaway Memorial Chapel was built by Gardens founder Cason J. Callaway, who dearly loved his mother and never forgot the indelible Christian influence she had on his life.

Callaway spent many afternoons on long walks through the woods, looking for the perfect spot to build the chapel. He pored over the plans for countless hours and personally directed every detail for what would become one of the most inspiring places in the Gardens. Just a week after the plans were finalized, Cason Callaway died, and although he never saw the chapel once it was built, he had seen it clearly in his mind's eye.

The quaint, 16th century, Gothic-style chapel is colored by a series of stained-glass windows that depict the forests and the various seasons. Regular concerts on the custom-built Moller organ fills the air around the chapel with beautiful music, providing an area perfect for reflection and meditation. Over the years, thousands of couples have taken their vows of marriage here, choosing the chapel for its beauty and simplicity.

Angel Biscuits

1	cake or package yeast	3	teaspoons baking powder
2	tablespoons lukewarm water	4	tablespoons sugar
		1	tablespoon salt
5	cups flour, sifted	1	cup shortening
1	teaspoon baking soda	2	cups buttermilk

Dissolve yeast in lukewarm water. Sift flour with other dry ingredients into a bowl. Cut in shortening. Add buttermilk, then yeast mixture. Stir until all flour is dampened. Knead on floured board about 2 minutes. Roll out to ½ inch thickness and cut with biscuit cutter. Bake at 450 degrees about 12 to 15 minutes.

This dough may be placed in refrigerator after mixing and used as needed. Biscuits may also be baked 7 minutes, frozen, and finish baking when ready to use.

Wonderful using country ham, for ham biscuits.

Yield: 40 biscuits

Cason and Virginia Callaway met at a party in Atlanta, and he knew this was the woman he would marry. On April 3, 1920, they were wed in her hometown of Pelham, Georgia. They had three children, Virginia ("Jinks"), Cason ("Caso") Jr., and Howard ("Bo").

Basic Biscuit

2	cups self-rising flour, sifted	⅔	cup buttermilk or sweet milk
3	tablespoons shortening		

Put flour into mixing bowl; cut in shortening with pastry cutter or mix well with hand. Slowly pour in milk and stir. Mixture will be thick enough to lift onto floured board to roll out to ½ inch thickness and cut with biscuit cutter. If you prefer, lightly flour hands and pinch off small amount of dough mixture. Roll into small round balls and mash into ovals ½ inch thick. Place on greased baking pan. Bake in 450 degree oven for 10 to 12 minutes.

Yield: 12 servings

Forbidden Biscuits

2	sticks margarine
1	(8 ounce) carton sour cream

2   cups self-rising flour, sifted

Melt butter and cool to lukewarm. It must be lukewarm or it will curdle the sour cream when mixed. Add lukewarm margarine to sour cream and mix well. Do not beat. Stir in flour. Drop by teaspoon into ungreased tiny muffin tins. Bake at 450 degrees for 10 to 15 minutes. These melt in your mouth.

Yield: 24 servings

Cason Callaway used his Blue Springs Farm to show that land could be farmed profitably. His experiments included the use of terracing and cover crops. In addition to growing strawberries, blueberries, muscadines, nuts, chickens, cattle, ducks, quail, pheasants and turkeys, the farm was also an experiment in food processing. Cason built dehydrating and canning plants to process his harvest.

Butterhorn Rolls

1	cup milk
½	cup shortening
1	package yeast
½	cup sugar

1	teaspoon salt
3	eggs, slightly beaten
4	cups flour, sifted

Scald milk and remove from heat. Add shortening. Combine yeast with sugar and add to lukewarm milk mixture. Add salt and eggs. Add flour and mix well. Let rise until double in size (2 to 3 hours). Place on floured board. Divide into 3 sections and roll each section into a circle about ¼ inch thick. Brush with melted butter and cut pie shape wedges. Beginning at the round edge, roll each wedge and place on greased pan with pointed end underneath. Brush top with melted butter and allow to rise until double in size. Bake in preheated 400 degree oven for 15 minutes.

Recipe may be doubled. Freezes well. Bake only 10 minutes if you plan to freeze.

Yield: 5 dozen small rolls

Sourdough Bread

Starter Recipe

1	package yeast	½	cup sugar
2	cups warm water	2	teaspoons salt
½	cup instant potatoes		

Dissolve yeast in ½ cup water; add remaining ingredients and stir well. Keep at room temperature for 24 hours. Cover with cloth and refrigerate. Your starter needs to be regulated (fed) every 3 to 5 days. When it is time to feed it, add the following:

¾	cup sugar	1	cup warm water
5	tablespoons instant potatoes		

Mix well and leave out of the refrigerator all day. Take out 1 cup to use in making bread and return remainder to the refrigerator in a cloth covered glass jar or bowl. Repeat every 3 to 5 days.

Bread Recipe

1	cup starter	5½-6	cups bread flour (must use bread flour)
½	cup vegetable oil		
1	tablespoon salt	½	cup sugar
1⅓	cups warm water		

Cason Callaway created the Georgia Better Farms program in which farmers were taught successful farming techniques. This innovative program resulted in profitable farms for almost all of its participants and helped improve the economic welfare of farmers across the state.

In a large bowl, combine these ingredients to make a stiff batter. Place ball of dough in a well oiled bowl and turn until entire ball is well oiled. Cover with wax paper and let rise overnight or until triple in size. The next morning, punch down dough and divide into 3 parts. Knead each part on a lightly floured surface. Very little kneading is necessary. Place each loaf into a greased 9x5 inch loaf pan. Brush with oil. Cover lightly and let rise 6 to 12 hours. Bake at 350 degrees for 30 to 35 minutes. Brush with butter. Let cool and remove from pan.

Yield: 3 loaves

Yeast Rolls

½	cup boiling water	1	egg, beaten
¼	cup sugar	1	package yeast
1	teaspoon salt	½	cup warm water
½	cup shortening	3	cups flour, unsifted

Mix water, sugar, salt and shortening. Let cool. Add egg. Dissolve yeast in warm water. Add to first mixture. Add flour and mix well. Cover and refrigerate overnight. Roll dough and cut out rolls with biscuit cutter. Roll each in melted butter. Place in pan with rolls touching. Let rise in warm place about 2 hours. Bake at 400 degrees 12 to 15 minutes until rolls brown on top.

Dough will keep several days in refrigerator.

Yield: 2½ dozen

Callaway Gardens could be referred to as the land of the lakes — more than a dozen in all! Virginia Callaway said her husband could never cross a stream without wanting to dam it and build a lake. The largest, Mountain Creek Lake, is 175 acres and is central in the Gardens so that all visitors are treated to its glistening waters. Most of the remaining lakes are named after birds — Chickadee, Whippoorwill, Robin, Hummingbird, Bluebird, Bobolink, Martin, Mockingbird, Thrasher, and Wren Lakes.

Popular Popovers

2	eggs	1	cup milk
1	cup all-purpose flour, sifted	½	teaspoon salt

Break eggs into bowl. Stir with fork. Add other ingredients. Mix well. Disregard lumps. Fill well-greased muffin tin (no papers, please) ¾ full. Place in cold oven. Set at 450 degrees; turn on heat and bake 30 minutes. (No peeking - they will fall). Reduce heat to 350 degrees for 5 minutes. Remove from tins and serve immediately.

Yield: 6 servings

Egg Bread

3	eggs	2	cups self-rising cornmeal
1	cup buttermilk	½	cup vegetable oil

Mix all ingredients together. Pour into greased baking pan. Bake at 350 degrees for 30 minutes.

Yield: 10 servings

Crackling Corn Bread

1 cup pork cracklings	1 teaspoon salt
½-1 cup hot water	Cold water sufficient for
2 cups cornmeal	stiff dough

Mash cracklings into small pieces; soak in hot water (you may need up to 1 cup) for 10 minutes. Pour into cornmeal and salt. Add enough cold water to make stiff dough; let stand for 5 minutes. If dough is too stiff, add more cold water. Shape into 2 pones, place into greased iron skillet or baking pan. Bake at 350 degrees until brown (about 30 minutes).

You may put cracklings into any kind of cornbread and bake as usual.

Yield: 8 servings

Golden Brown Buttermilk Cornbread

2¼ cups self-rising buttermilk	1 cup evaporated milk
cornmeal mix	½ cup water
1 teaspoon sugar	¾ cup vegetable oil
1 large yellow onion, chopped	1 egg
(optional)	½ stick margarine

Combine the first 7 ingredients; mixing well. Pour batter into an 8 inch round pan that is well greased with vegetable shortening. Bake in preheated 425 degree oven for 30 to 35 minutes or until golden brown. Remove bread from oven and lightly punch holes in entire top of bread with a dinner fork. Melt margarine and pour over the top of the bread. Remove bread from pan immediately by inverting on serving plate. Cut into 8 wedges and cover serving plate with foil or plastic wrap until ready to serve.

Yield: 8 servings

Various shaped cast iron pans are a popular item in the Callaway Country Store. To season a pan follow these steps: Wash new pans with soap and water. Dry well. Rub inside and outside of pan with melted vegetable shortening. Bake in 350 degree oven for one hour. Let pan cool inside the oven. Rub pan lightly with vegetable oil, wipe dry and store. After use, clean with hot water and a brush. Always dry immediately. Occasionally clean with soap and water, then re-season. Re-seasoning is necessary after cooking acidic foods.

Quick Muffin Rolls

| 2 | cups self-rising flour | 1 | cup milk |
| 4 | tablespoons mayonnaise | 1 | teaspoon sugar |

Mix all ingredients together for 2 minutes. Pour into greased 12 cup muffin pan. Bake 10 minutes or until golden brown at 450 degrees.

Yield: 12 servings

Virginia Callaway was a true conservationist at heart. When Canada geese discovered Callaway Gardens and insisted on making their home in this wildlife refuge, Virginia had a manmade island placed in the middle of a lake so the geese would be safe from predators. Today, that island in Hummingbird Lake is still a favorite place for geese to raise their goslings.

Basic Dumplings

| 2 | cups all-purpose flour | 3 | tablespoons shortening |
| ½ | teaspoon salt | ⅔ | cup milk |

Combine flour and salt; cut in shortening until mixture resembles coarse meal. Add milk to make stiff dough. Place dough on a well floured surface, roll thin. Cut into strips or squares.

May be used in stews or pot pies

To freeze, place strips or squares on cookie sheet. Put in freezer until frozen; then place into freezer bags and take out to use as needed.

Yield: 8 servings

Sally Lunn

2	cups milk	1½	cakes yeast
4	tablespoons sugar	3	eggs, beaten
2	teaspoons salt	6	cups flour
1	cup shortening		

Scald milk, add sugar, salt and shortening. Cool to lukewarm and crumble in the yeast. Stir in beaten eggs. Add flour and beat thoroughly. Cover and let rise until double in bulk. Place in ring mold or tube pan. Let rise again until double in bulk. Bake at 350 degrees for 1 hour.

Yield: 16 servings

Spoonbread

½ cup self-rising cornmeal
2 cups milk (hot, not boiling)
½ teaspoon salt

4 egg yolks, beaten
4 egg whites, beaten stiff

Make a mush of meal, milk and salt. Cook until thick. Add beaten egg yolks, then fold in beaten egg whites. Pour into 1½ quart casserole or soufflé dish. Bake at 325 degrees for 45 minutes. Serve with melted butter to pour over.

Yield: 6 servings

Hush Puppies

1½ cups cornmeal
½ cup all-purpose flour
1 teaspoon baking soda
1 teaspoon baking powder
½ teaspoon salt

1 large egg, beaten
1½-2 cups buttermilk
6 tablespoons chopped onion
    (optional)

Mix all dry ingredients. Add egg, buttermilk and onion. Mix thoroughly. Drop by tablespoon into deep, hot fat. When done, they will float. Drain on paper towels. Delicious served with fish (especially fried catfish).

Yield: 10 servings

The Gardens and Veranda Restaurants are housed in the original Clubhouse. In the early years, Cason and his guests enjoyed visiting as they sat on its grand two-tiered porch that overlooks the Lake View Golf Course and Mountain Creek Lake. Today, restaurant patrons may enjoy their meals on the Gardens Restaurant porch while enjoying the picturesque view.

Date Nut Bread

2 cups dates, cut in large
    chunks
½ teaspoon salt
1 teaspoon baking soda
1 tablespoon butter or
    margarine

1 cup boiling water
1 egg
1 cup sugar
2 cups flour
1 cup chopped walnuts

Preheat oven to 350 degrees. Place dates in medium bowl. Sprinkle salt and soda over dates and add butter. Pour 1 cup boiling water over all and set aside. Beat egg, add sugar. Add flour alternately with the liquid from dates. Add dates and nuts. Spoon into greased and floured 9x5 loaf pan. Bake at 350 degrees about 1 hour.

Yield: 12 servings

Lemon Bread

½	cup shortening	½	cup milk
1½	cups sugar, divided	½	teaspoon lemon extract
2	eggs	1	teaspoon lemon peel
1½	cups all-purpose flour	½	cup chopped nuts
1	teaspoon baking powder		Juice of one lemon
¼	teaspoon salt		

The Callaway Country Store was built as an outlet for the products from Blue Springs Farms. It was built on Highway 27 which was the main route for all traffic in and out of Florida. Today, its popularity remains as shoppers find unique gift and home decor items. But the most popular purchases are the gourmet food products including Speckled Heart Grits and the delicious muscadine products.

Preheat oven to 350 degrees. Grease 5x9 inch loaf pan. Cream shortening with 1¼ cup sugar; mix in eggs. Sift flour with baking powder and salt. Alternately add the flour mixture and the milk to shortening mixture, beginning and ending with flour. Mix in lemon extract, peel and nuts. Bake in 5x9 inch loaf pan for 1 hour at 350 degrees. Combine remaining ¼ cup sugar and lemon juice and pour over the top of the loaf when it comes from the oven. You can poke a few holes in the top of the loaf before pouring the juice over if you wish. If you combine the sugar and juice just before pouring you will get a crisp, sugary topping rather than a glaze.

Yield: 12 servings

❋ Callaway Gardens Muscadine Bread

½	cup butter	½	cup milk
1	cup sugar	½	cup Callaway Gardens
2	eggs		Muscadine Sauce®
2	cups flour	½	cup chopped pecans
1½	teaspoons baking powder		

Preheat oven to 325 degrees. Cream butter and sugar until light and fluffy. Add eggs, beating in one at a time. Sift dry ingredients together and add alternately with the milk and Muscadine sauce. Stir in nuts. Bake in greased and floured 5x9 inch loaf pan at 325 degrees for approximately 50 to 60 minutes until toothpick inserted in the center comes out clean.

Yield: 12 servings

Pear Bread

3 cups all-purpose flour	¾ cup oil
1 teaspoon baking soda	3 eggs, slightly beaten
¼ teaspoon baking powder	2 cups sugar
1 teaspoon salt	2 cups peeled and grated
1 tablespoon ground	pears
cinnamon	2 teaspoons vanilla
1 cup chopped nuts	

Preheat oven to 325 degrees. Combine all dry ingredients. Combine all liquid ingredients. Add the liquid ingredients to the dry. Mix until ingredients are moistened. Spoon mixture into 2 (9¼x5¼x2¾ inch) loaf pans. Bake 1 hour at 325 degrees or until bread tests done.

Yield: 2 loaves

Callaway Gardens opened on May 21, 1952 as Ida Cason Gardens, named after Cason's beloved mother. The name was changed to Ida Cason Callaway Gardens in 1955 and, finally to Callaway Gardens in 1961. It's not unusual to hear old-timers still refer to it as "Ida Cason's."

Poppy Seed Loaves

3 cups flour	2¼ cups sugar
1½ teaspoons salt	1½ teaspoons vanilla
1½ teaspoons baking powder	1½ teaspoons almond extract
3 eggs	1½ teaspoons butter flavoring
1½ cups milk	1½ teaspoons poppy seeds
1½ cups oil	

Glaze

½ teaspoon butter flavoring	¼ cup orange juice
½ teaspoon almond flavoring	¾ cup granulated sugar
½ teaspoon vanilla	

Preheat oven to 350 degrees. Mix ingredients for one to two minutes with electric beater. Put into two lightly greased 9x5 inch loaf pans. Bake at 350 degrees for 1 hour. Mix glaze and pour over warm bread.

Yield: 2 loaves

Strawberry Bread Supreme

3	cups all-purpose flour	1	cup vegetable oil
2	cups sugar	2	(10 ounce) packages frozen
1	teaspoon baking soda		strawberries, thawed
1	teaspoon ground cinnamon	1	cup chopped pecans
1	teaspoon salt		(optional)
4	eggs, beaten		

Glaze

½	cup powdered sugar	Reserved strawberry juice

In large bowl, stir by hand the flour, sugar, baking soda, cinnamon and salt. Then mix in eggs and oil. Drain strawberries and reserve juice. Stir in drained strawberries and pecans. Pour into 2 large or 4 mini loaf pans. Bake at 350 degrees for 1 hour for large loaves or 45 to 50 minutes for small loaves, or until toothpick inserted in the center comes out clean. Cool on rack. For glaze, gradually mix juice into sugar and pour on top of loaves.

Yield: 2 large or 4 mini loaves

Robin Lake Beach is the longest manmade white sand beach in the world. The one-mile long beach opened in 1953, two years after the Gardens opened.

Zucchini Bread

4	eggs	¾	teaspoon baking powder
2	cups sugar	2	cups grated zucchini
1	cup vegetable oil	1	cup chopped walnuts or
3½	cups flour		pecans
1½	teaspoons baking soda	1	cup raisins
1½	teaspoons salt	1	teaspoon vanilla
1	teaspoon cinnamon		

In large bowl, beat eggs; gradually beat in sugar and oil. Combine dry ingredients and add to the first mixture, alternating with zucchini. Stir in raisins, nuts and vanilla. Put in greased and floured 4x8 inch bread pans. Bake at 350 degrees for 55 minutes. Freezes well.

Yield: 2 loaves

Irish Soda Bread

2½	cups all-purpose flour	3	tablespoons butter, softened
½	teaspoon salt	½	cup buttermilk, use up to
1	teaspoon baking powder		¾ cup
1	teaspoon baking soda	⅓	cup raisins (optional)

Preheat oven to 375 degrees. Combine dry ingredients and cut in butter until mixture resembles fine bread crumbs. (If using raisins, stir them in now.) Add enough buttermilk to make a soft dough. On a lightly floured surface, knead for 1 or 2 minutes until smooth. Shape into a 6 to 7 inch round. Place on a greased cookie sheet; cut a cross about ¼ of the way down into the loaf starting almost at the edge of the round. Bake in a 375 degree preheated oven until golden brown.

Irish Soda Bread is nice, and not just for St. Patrick's Day, but all year and makes a great fall or winter tea with butter and jam. If this is to be for a tea, raisins make it better.

Yield: 8 servings

Although Cason closed his Blue Springs Farm, he never got completely away from farming. His last major project was a 7.5-acre demonstration garden named affectionately, Mr. Cason's Garden. The garden features an extensive herb garden, vegetables, fruits, flowers, and an All America Trial Garden. It is also home to the Southern filming site of the popular PBS television series, The Victory Garden.

Blueberry-Lemon Muffins

1¾	cups all-purpose flour	⅓	cup vegetable oil
½	cup sugar	1	cup fresh or frozen
2½	teaspoons baking powder		blueberries
½	teaspoon salt	2	tablespoons sugar
¾	cup milk	1	teaspoon grated lemon rind
1	egg, beaten	1	teaspoon lemon juice

Preheat oven to 400 degrees. In medium bowl, combine flour, ½ cup sugar, baking powder and salt. Make a well in the center of the flour mixture. In another small bowl, combine milk, beaten egg and vegetable oil. Pour into flour mixture and mix until just moist. Toss together blueberries, 2 tablespoons sugar, lemon rind and lemon juice. Gently fold into batter. Spoon mixture into greased muffin tins to ¾ full. Bake 20 to 25 minutes until golden brown.

Yield: 12 muffins

English Scones with Strawberry Lemon Balm Butter

English Scones

2	cups all-purpose flour	½	cup margarine
1	tablespoon sugar	⅔	cup milk
1	teaspoon baking soda	1	egg yolk, beaten
1	teaspoon cream of tartar	1	tablespoon water

Strawberry Lemon Balm Butter

1	cup unsalted butter	⅓	cup finely chopped straw-berries
3	tablespoons powdered sugar	2	tablespoons chopped lemon balm

Sift flour, sugar, baking soda and cream of tartar together. Cut in margarine until coarse and resembles soft breadcrumbs. Stir in milk to make soft dough. Divide into two portions. Pat out on floured board into a round, ¾ inch thick. Cut across making four pie-shaped sections or use cutter to make individual rounds of desired size. Put shapes onto baking sheet. Beat egg yolk and water together to make egg wash. Brush on top of dough. Bake at 400 degrees for 10 to 12 minutes. Meanwhile, prepare balm butter by pulsing butter and sugar in food processor. Add remaining ingredients and pulse. Split scone and butter generously.

If scones are made ahead, reheat when needed by wrapping in foil and heating in 300 degree oven for several minutes.

Strawberry Lemon Balm Butter is also delicious on biscuits, fruit muffins and waffles.

Yield: 16 scones and 1⅓ cups butter

Guests to Callaway Gardens are transported back in time when they stop by the Pioneer Log Cabin in the Meadowlark Area. The two-room cabin, built in the late 1800s, was home to a family of 15. A hostess in period costume greets visitors to the dwelling and explains the daily rigors of life in the 1800s.

Eggs, Cheese
and Breakfast
Dishes

The Trails at Callaway Gardens

Go take a hike...

   ... is an invitation to enjoy the splendor of Mother Nature at Callaway Gardens. Miles of nature trails beckon visitors to part from the main road and take a beaten path where flowers and wildlife flourish. The Mountain Creek Lake Trail, Azalea Trail, Laurel Springs Trail, Wildflower Trail, Holly Trail, Rhododendron Trail and Azalea Bowl Trail each have their own discoveries awaiting inquisitive hikers. Special collections, native plants, a hardwood forest, and Georgia's rare, endangered and protected plants are some of what you'll find growing along these lovely paths. Because of the flora that changes each season, trails merit visits throughout the year.

   So, the next time someone bids you to go take a hike, take them up on it and explore one of Callaway Gardens' trails.

 *Callaway Family Recipes*

Freezer French Toast

4	eggs	8	slices day old French bread,
1	cup milk		cut into ¾ inch slices
2	tablespoons sugar		Melted butter
1	teaspoon vanilla		Powdered sugar, honey or
⅛	teaspoon coriander		syrup

Beat together eggs, milk, sugar, vanilla and coriander. Place bread slices in a rimmed baking sheet. Pour egg mixture over bread and let stand for a few minutes. Turn slices over and let stand until all egg mixture is absorbed. Freeze, uncovered, until firm. Transfer to a plastic bag and return to freezer. To serve, place desired number of frozen slices on a greased baking sheet. Brush with melted butter and cover with foil. Bake in a 500 degree oven for 8 minutes. Turn slices over, brush with melted butter and bake for 10 minutes longer. Serve with powdered sugar, honey or syrup.

Yield: 8 servings

Maybe the best way to work up an appetite at Callaway Gardens is pedaling your way around the Discovery Bicycle Trail. Ten paved miles wind through the woods and past all the major attractions, giving bicyclists an opportunity to explore the plants and wildlife.

Baked Cinnamon French Toast

½	loaf French bread cut in 1 inch slices	¼	teaspoon nutmeg
		½	stick butter or margarine, softened
6	large eggs		
1½	cups milk	½	cup firmly packed brown sugar
1	cup half-and-half		
1	teaspoon vanilla extract	½	cups chopped nuts
¼	teaspoon cinnamon	1	tablespoon light corn syrup

The night before, butter 9x13 inch baking dish. Arrange bread slices, overlapping, in a single layer to fill bottom of dish. In medium bowl, combine eggs, milk, cream, vanilla, cinnamon and nutmeg; mix well. Pour over bread slices. Cover and refrigerate overnight. In the morning, preheat oven to 350 degrees. In a small bowl combine butter, brown sugar, nuts and corn syrup; spread over bread. Bake 40 minutes. Serve warm, topped with maple syrup.

Yield: 6 servings

Saturday Morning Pancakes

2¼ cups sifted all-purpose flour	1½ teaspoons salt
3 teaspoons baking powder	2 eggs, slightly beaten
1½ tablespoons sugar	2 cups milk
	4 tablespoons melted butter

Sift dry ingredients together. Break eggs in large bowl and beat slightly. Stir in milk and melted butter. Add sifted dry ingredients all at once. Stir only until flour is moistened. Do not beat. Heat oiled griddle or frying pan. Pour batter for size desired. Cook and enjoy.

Bacon pancakes: Break 8 slices crisp cooked bacon into small bits and add to batter.

Pecan pancakes: Fold ¾ cup chopped pecans into batter.

Blueberry pancakes: Fold ¾ cup blueberries into batter.

Yield: 6 servings

Eggs Benedict

6 English muffins	12 poached eggs
Butter	2 cups Hollandaise sauce
12 slices Canadian bacon	12 truffles, sliced (optional)

Hollandaise Sauce

5 eggs	½ cup butter
3 tablespoons hot water	Salt and white pepper to
2 tablespoons lemon juice	taste

Eggs Benedict: Split, butter and warm muffins. Layer muffin, ham, egg, sauce and truffle slice. Hollandaise sauce: In a large mixing bowl, beat the egg yolks with a wire whisk until they are thick and pale in color. Add the water and lemon juice and beat vigorously. Heat the butter until it is just bubbly and pour it slowly into the egg mixture, beating as it is added. Pour the mixture into a saucepan. Cook over a very low heat, stirring constantly, until the sauce thickens. (About 10 minutes). Season to taste with salt and white pepper. Serve immediately. Hungry eaters may want two servings.

If the sauce begins to curdle, remove from the heat and beat in 2 tablespoons light cream. The sauce may be kept warm over hot (but not boiling) water for 15 to 20 minutes before serving.

Yield: 12 servings, 1 cup sauce

Fourth-graders were special to Virginia Callaway, who loved to open these young eyes to the world around them. She would take all fourth grade students in the county on a guided tour of the 3,000-acre Cason J. Callaway Memorial Forest, helping them discover the important role each person has in protecting our environment. The traditional fourth grade Memorial Forest hike is still enjoyed by the area's students and is led by Callaway Gardens naturalists.

Eggs Hussard

2	large, grilled thin slices of ham	2	slices grilled tomato
2	Holland rusks or 1 split English muffin	2	soft poached eggs
¼	cup Marchande de Vin sauce	¾	cup Hollandaise sauce Paprika

Marchande de Vin Sauce

¾	cup butter	½	teaspoon salt
⅓	cup minced ham	½	teaspoon pepper
⅓	cup finely chopped shallots		Dash cayenne pepper
½	cup finely chopped onion	¾	cup beef broth
2	tablespoons minced garlic	½	cup red wine
2	tablespoons all-purpose flour		

Eggs Hussard: Lay slice of ham across each Holland rusk or split muffin. Cover with Marchande de Vin sauce. Add slice of tomato, then the egg. Top with Hollandaise sauce and sprinkle with paprika. To prepare Marchande de Vin Sauce, melt butter in a 9 inch skillet. Add next four ingredients. Sauté until slightly brown. Add flour, salt, pepper and cayenne pepper. Cook until brown. Blend in beef broth and wine and simmer over low heat for 35 to 40 minutes.

This can be done ahead of serving time. The sauce may also be served with cheese grits.

Yield: 2 servings, 2 cups sauce (enough for 6 servings)

Scrambled Eggs

3	eggs	¼	cup chopped green pepper
1	teaspoon finely chopped rosemary	¼	cup chopped red pepper
1	teaspoon water	¼	cup sliced mushrooms
2	pats margarine	1	slice processed cheese or
1	slice onion, finely chopped		⅛ cup grated cheddar cheese

Beat together eggs, rosemary and water. Set aside. In a small skillet, melt the margarine and lightly sauté all of the other ingredients, except cheese. Beat eggs again and add to skillet mixture, scrambling lightly. Add cheese at the end, just to melt slightly. Serve immediately.

Yield: 2 servings

The Cecil B. Day Butterfly Center is one of North America's largest glass-enclosed tropical butterfly conservatories. It is home to 1,000 butterflies that flutter freely in a tropical setting of lush foliage. Visitors to the Center can see a butterfly emerge from a chrysalis, learn about the life cycles of these colorful insects by watching the award-winning film, On Wings of Wonder, *and take home a butterfly-related souvenir from the Gift Shop.*

Ramekin Cheese and Egg Bake

2	tablespoons butter, melted	6	eggs
1	cup shredded cheddar cheese	6	tablespoons half-and-half
2	green onions with tops, sliced		Salt, pepper and paprika

Preheat oven to 325 degrees. Grease 6 ramekin or custard cups with the butter using a brush. Divide green onions and half the cheese equally in the cups. With care, break the egg onto the cheese in the cup; pour 1 tablespoon half-and-half on each egg. Season with salt, pepper, paprika and add remaining cheese evenly divided. Cook uncovered in 325 degree oven for 20 minutes until white is set, yolks still soft. While these are cooking, prepare rest of breakfast. Garnish with sprig of parsley.

Yield: 6 servings

The Callaway Brothers Azalea Bowl, opened March 1999, is a tribute to brothers Fuller E. Callaway Sr. and Ely Callaway Sr. Fuller was the father of Cason J. Callaway, founder of the Gardens; Ely was the father of Ely Callaway Jr., founder of Callaway Golf. The Azalea Bowl is actually a year-round garden that features 40 acres of azaleas and a wide collection of native plants and trees. A babbling stream, reflection pond, paved walking trail and arched bridge add interesting highlights to this inviting garden.

Bridge Club Cheese Strata

12	slices bread	2	cups finely diced ham, or cooked sausage
¾	pound shredded sharp cheddar cheese	6	eggs, slightly beaten
1	(10 ounce) package frozen broccoli, cooked and drained	3½	cups milk
		2	tablespoons minced onion
		½	teaspoon salt
		¼	teaspoon dry mustard

Prepare the day before. Cut 12 doughnuts and holes out of bread. Set aside. Fit scraps into bottom of a 9x13 inch pan. Place cheese in a layer over the bread. Add a layer of broccoli, then ham. Arrange bread doughnuts and holes over top. Combine remaining ingredients, pour over bread in casserole. Refrigerate overnight or at least 6 hours. Bake uncovered in slow oven, 325 degrees, for 55 minutes. For a pretty finish, sprinkle with shredded cheese 5 minutes before end of baking time. Let stand 10 minutes. Cut into squares, and serve.

Yield: 12 servings

Welsh Rarebit

1	tablespoon butter	1	teaspoon salt
1	cup beer		Dash red pepper
1	pound shredded New York	½-¾	cup cream (optional)
	extra sharp cheddar cheese		Unbuttered toast
1	egg		Tomato (optional)
¼	teaspoon dry mustard		

Melt butter in double boiler; add beer. When hot, blend in cheese, stirring constantly until cheese is melted. Slightly beat the egg and add to mixture together with seasonings. If adding cream, do it slowly, stirring constantly. Serve over unbuttered hot toast.

Serve thick slices of grilled tomatoes on top of toast, cover with the rarebit, and garnish with bacon.

Yield: 8 servings

Party Cheese Soufflé

4½	cups milk	2	teaspoons salt
1	scant cup instant tapioca	14	eggs, separated
4½	cups grated cheese	15	slices cooked bacon
			Paprika and parsley flakes

Sauce

1½	sticks margarine	3	cups milk, scalded
⅓	cup flour	2½	cups grated cheddar cheese

Cook milk and tapioca until thick. Add cheese and stir until cheese is melted. Stir in beaten egg yolks and salt. Beat egg whites until stiff. Fold into mixture carefully (do no stir). Put in a buttered 9x13 inch casserole. Place in a pan of water and bake in a 300 degree oven for 1½ hours or until firm. Sauce: Combine margarine, flour and milk as for a cream sauce. Add cheese and stir constantly until melted. Presentation: Cut soufflé into 15 square pieces. Lift each piece carefully onto a plate. Place 2 half slices of bacon on each square. Put a generous spoon of sauce on each square. Sprinkle with paprika and parsley flakes.

This recipe will never fall. Half the recipe may be prepared. Excellent for brunch.

Yield: 15 servings

The Virginia Hand Callaway Discovery Center opened in February 2000 in honor of the Gardens' co-founder. The 35,000-square-foot facility is the perfect place to discover what the Gardens offers, as well as to learn about our natural environment. The Center includes an orientation theater, auditorium, exhibit hall, education wing and the Mountain Creek Cafe. The centerpiece of the lobby is a life-size bronze statue of Virginia Callaway and her Great Dane, Rex Muddynose.

Tomato and Blue Cheese Tart

1	(10 inch) pie shell	1	pint whipping cream	
2	tablespoons minced shallots	¾	teaspoon salt	
2	medium tomatoes, peeled and sliced	¼	teaspoon freshly ground pepper	
12	ounces crumbled blue cheese	4	large eggs, lightly whisked	

Preheat oven to 350 degrees. Place tomatoes on paper towels and pat dry. On bottom of the pie shell, sprinkle shallots and cover evenly with tomatoes and then cheese. Combine other ingredients and blend well. Pour into pie shell. Place in preheated oven and bake 35 to 40 minutes until puffy and light brown. This will be easier to handle if you slide it onto a cookie sheet to remove it. Do not over bake.

Yield: 8 servings

Hot Deviled Eggs

12	large eggs, hard-boiled
12	thin slices ham, baked or broiled
	Soft butter or mayonnaise

Worcestershire sauce (optional)
Mustard (optional)
Salt and pepper (red or white), to taste

Sauce

1	can mushroom soup
¼	cup water
1½	cups grated cheese
2	tablespoons ripe olives, pitted

Curry powder (optional)
Dry white wine (optional)
Potato chips

Halve the eggs. Mash egg yolks with soft butter or mayonnaise, salt, pepper and a few drops of Worcestershire sauce or mustard. (However you like to season them). Stuff back into the whites. Put two halves back together and wrap with thin slice of ham. Place in a shallow casserole and cover with sauce. To prepare sauce, dilute soup with water, add grated cheese, ripe olives chopped into large pieces and season with a little curry powder or dry white wine. Top with crushed potato chips. Bake uncovered at 350 degrees for 25 minutes.

Good served with sherried fruits and stuffed fresh mushrooms.

Yield: 12 servings

Lights, lights, lights ...it must be Fantasy In Lights®, the holiday tradition of the South! This extraordinary outdoor light show started in 1992 with four major scenes and an outdoor Christmas Village. Since then it has grown to include more than a dozen lighted scenes complete with music and animation, and a 22,000-square foot, heated, indoor Christmas Village. Each year, approximately a quarter of a million people spend an evening viewing the lights and getting in the spirit of the season.

Deviled Eggs

6	eggs, hard-boiled	½	teaspoon dry mustard
2	tablespoons mayonnaise	1	teaspoon prepared mustard
1	teaspoon vinegar		Salt and pepper
¼	teaspoon paprika		

Halve hard-boiled eggs lengthwise; remove yolks and mash with desired combination of seasonings. Refill egg whites.

Mash yolks with 2 tablespoons mayonnaise, 1 tablespoon horse-radish, 1 tablespoon chopped sweet pickles, salt to taste and paprika for garnishing.

Use parsley, chopped onions or chives, or finely chopped celery mixed with the yolks and mayonnaise.

Yield: 12 servings

Cheese Soufflé for Six

3	tablespoons butter	1	teaspoon prepared mustard
¼	cup flour	2	drops Worcestershire sauce
1⅞	cups milk	1	cup American cheese,
	Salt to taste		grated and packed
	Dash cayenne pepper	6	eggs, separated

Make a cream sauce by melting the butter and blending in the flour. Cook until bubbly. Add the milk, salt, cayenne , mustard, Worcestershire and bring to a boil, stirring constantly. Boil 1 minute, time it. Remove from heat and cool slightly. Add the cheese. Beat egg yolks until thick and add to cheese mixture, stirring constantly. Beat egg whites until stiff. Fold into the cheese mixture, carefully. Pour into a well buttered baking dish, ¾ full. Bake at 300 degrees in a hot-water bath for 2 hours or until a silver knife inserted into the center comes out clean.

This soufflé will keep a day in the refrigerator after baking so it can be a successful leftover. Use as a base for Chicken Oriental, à la king foods or any creamed dish.

Yield: 6 servings

The Florida State University "Flying High" Circus has made Callaway Gardens its summer home since 1960. Approximately 25 of the college's top circus performers are invited to Callaway Gardens each summer to perform under the Big Top and to serve as day camp counselors for the popular Summer Family Adventure program.

Grits Soufflé

2½ cups milk
½   cup grits
3   eggs, separated
1   teaspoon salt

½   teaspoon baking powder
½   teaspoon sugar
2   tablespoons butter, melted

Scald milk, do not boil, and add grits. Cook until thick. Beat egg yolks and add to grits with salt, baking powder, sugar and melted butter. Beat egg whites to a soft peak and fold into batter. Pour into well-buttered 1½ quart casserole and bake uncovered at 375 degrees for 25 to 30 minutes.

Yield: 8 servings

If you ask six Southern ladies how to cook grits you will get six different recipes. Following are some of our favorites. You will find another, entitled Shrimp and Grits, with the fish recipes.

Callaway Gardens Baked Grits Soufflé

1½ cups Speckled Heart
        Grits®
4½ cups water
2   cans mushroom soup

6   eggs, well beaten
2   cups grated sharp cheddar
        cheese
1   cup cracker crumbs

Add Speckled Heart grits to 4½ cups boiling water. Bring to a second boil, reduce heat to medium, cover and cook 25 to 30 minutes, stirring often to prevent sticking. Mix with mushroom soup. Add eggs. Place mixture in baking dish greased with bacon drippings. Cover with cracker crumbs and cheese. Bake at 400 degrees for 30 minutes.

Yield: 8 to 10 servings

Callaway Gardens Speckled Heart Grits

4	cups boiling water	1	teaspoon salt
1	cup Callaway Gardens Speckled Heart Grits®		

Bring water to a boil, add grits and salt, reduce heat to medium, cover and cook for about 20 to 30 minutes, stirring often to prevent sticking. Additional water may be added for the desired consistency, as the grits cook. The addition of milk instead of water at this point gives a delightful creamy quality to the grits. Serve hot with plenty of butter or margarine, or with gravy.

The grits may be cooked in a double boiler, which takes a little longer, but eliminates stirring so often.

Yield: 4 servings

With 63 holes of golf, Callaway Gardens is a great place to tee off. Three 18-hole courses and an executive 9-hole course provide plenty of challenge. The Mountain View golf course is home to the PGA Tour's Buick Challenge each autumn when some of the world's greatest golfers meet to compete.

Callaway Gardens Cheese Grits

1	cup Speckled Heart Grits®	2	cups sharp grated cheese
4	cups water	1	stick margarine
1	teaspoon salt		Dash hot pepper sauce

Cook grits according to traditional recipe above. Combine all ingredients, pour in casserole dish, bake 1 hour at 325 degrees.

Yield: 4 to 6 servings

Cheese Grits

1	cup grits	½	teaspoon salt
4	cups boiling water	2	eggs
½	pound American cheese		

Cook grits with water in double boiler for 30 minutes, until they reach pouring consistency. Grate 2 tablespoons cheese to sprinkle on top; set aside. Cut up remainder of cheese and stir into hot grits until melted. Add salt to taste. Beat eggs until very light and add to warm (not hot) grits. Prepare casserole with thick coating of butter. Pour mixture in, sprinkling top with cheese. Set in a pan of water and bake in preheated 325 degree oven for 20 to 25 minutes. Serve immediately.

Substitute milk for the water and 1 roll garlic cheese, cubed, for the American cheese. Scald 3½ cups milk. Add grits, simmer 25 minutes. Remove from heat and add eggs, remaining ½ cup milk, ½ cup butter and cheese.

Yield: 8 servings

Down South Cheese Grits

4	cups water	1½	cups shredded cheddar cheese
1	cup quick cooking grits		
1	teaspoon salt	1	cup milk
4	eggs, slightly beaten	1	stick butter
			Dash cayenne pepper

Bring water to boil in a large sauce pan; add salt. Gradually stir in grits and cook, stirring occasionally, for 4 to 5 minutes. Remove from heat; stir in slightly beaten eggs, 1 cup shredded cheddar cheese, milk, butter and pepper. Pour mixture into a buttered 1 quart baking dish. Sprinkle remaining ½ cup shredded cheese over top of casserole. Bake in 350 degree oven for 1 hour.

Yield: 8 servings

The perfect vacation isn't so hard to find. Since 1960, families have delighted themselves with Summer Family Adventure, the vacation plan that has something for everyone. "Adventurers" spend a week in a Callaway cottage and are treated to an endless schedule of activities including a day camp for the children. While the children are having the time of their lives at camp, parents enjoy the activities of their choice — and everyone's having fun! In the evenings, activities are planned for the entire family. By the end of the week, no one wants to go home!

Garlic Cheese Grits

1 cup grits	½ cup butter
4 cups milk, divided	1 roll garlic cheese, chopped
2 eggs, beaten	into cubes

Bring 3½ cups milk just to a boil. Add grits, reduce heat and simmer approximately 25 minutes or until done. Remove from heat. Add eggs, ½ cup milk, butter and cheese. Pour into a 2 quart casserole. Bake at 350 degrees for 25 minutes.

Substitute ½ teaspoon garlic powder and ½ cup shredded sharp cheese for the garlic cheese.

Yield: 8 servings

Yellow Cheese Grits

1 cup grits	1½ cups sharp cheddar cheese
4 cups boiling water	1 teaspoon salt
1 medium onion, minced	6 drops hot pepper sauce
1 stick butter (do not substitute)	1 egg, separated

Cook grits in boiling water for 25 to 30 minutes; add onion, butter, cheese, salt, pepper sauce and egg yolk. Cool completely. Beat egg whites until fluffy and fold into cooled grits. Pour into a 2 quart casserole and bake, uncovered, for 1 hour at 350 degrees. This will brown on top.

Yield: 6 servings

Callaway Gardens' Mountain Creek Villas put you in the lap of luxury. These exquisite vacation homes feature a spacious living area with a fireplace, fully-equipped kitchen, dining area, bedrooms with private bathrooms, washer and dryer, screened porch, and all the comforts of home.

Phenix City Slices

Leftover cheese grits   1   **cup flour**
1   **egg, beaten**   2   **tablespoons butter**

Place left over cheese grits in refrigerator in a loaf pan. Chill. Remove chilled grits from pan and cut into 1 inch thick slices. Dip slices in beaten egg and then in flour. Brown in buttered skillet.

Yield: 10 servings

Tomato Gravy

3   **tablespoons bacon drip-**   2   **medium (or 3 small) fresh**
    pings   **tomatoes, chopped**
2   **tablespoons flour**   **Salt and pepper to taste**

Heat the bacon drippings in an 8 to 10 inch frying pan (Best if made in the pan where your breakfast bacon has been fried). Add the flour and stir until lightly browned; then add the chopped tomatoes and stir until thickened. If it becomes too thick, add small amount of water to thin to a gravy consistency. Serve over grits with breakfast eggs and bacon or sausage.

Yield: 4 servings

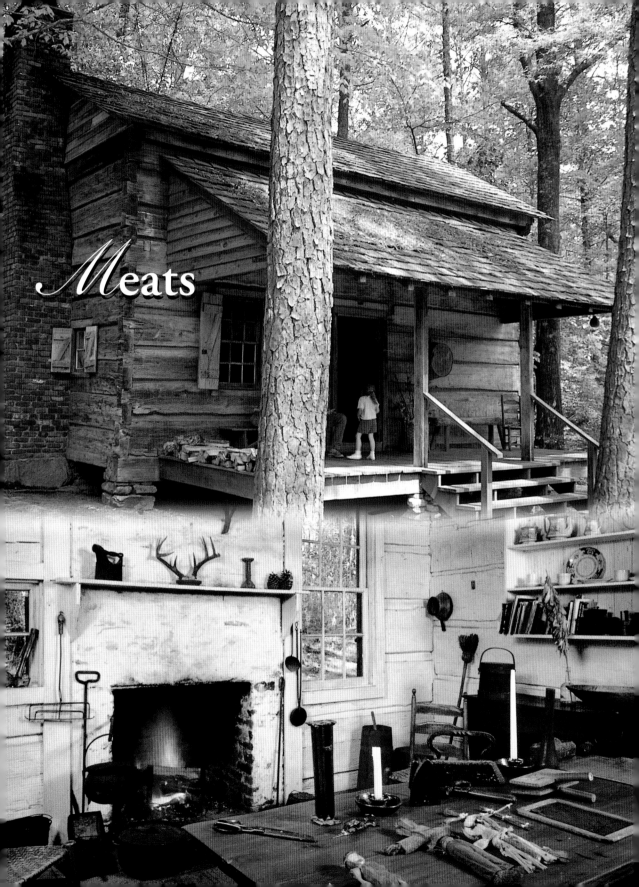

Meats

The Pioneer Log Cabin

It's like stepping back in time...

...when you step into the Pioneer Log Cabin at Callaway Gardens. This authentic dwelling was built during the 1830s and was inhabited for 100 years. The last family to live in it had 15 members!

Today, visitors are greeted by a pioneer in period costume, who may be stoking up the fire to start a pan of made-from-scratch biscuits. Life was hard in the 1800s and the living conditions were rugged, especially by today's standards. The cabin contains original and reproductions of the furnishings and implements needed by pioneers to survive daily life.

The cabin serves as a reminder of the persistence and courage of our pioneer forefathers and of how far our society has come in 200 years.

Callaway Family Recipes

Meat Loaf

1½ pounds lean ground beef
½ pound ground pork
1 large onion, finely chopped
1½ teaspoons salt
¼ teaspoon pepper
2 stalks celery, diced (optional)
½ small red bell pepper, diced (optional)

2 large eggs, beaten
1 cup bread crumbs, plain or cracker meal
2 (8 ounce) cans tomato sauce, divided
½ cup water
2 teaspoons Worcestershire sauce

Mix together first 9 ingredients and ½ can tomato sauce. Form into loaf. Place in shallow 7x10 inch baking pan. Combine water, Worcestershire sauce and remaining tomato sauce. Pour over loaf. Bake in 350 degree oven for 1 hour and 15 minutes, basting occasionally.

Yield: 8 servings

Sweet and Sour Meatloaf

1½ pounds ground beef
1 (8 ounce) can tomato sauce
1 egg, beaten
1 cup bread crumbs

¼ cup chopped onion
1 teaspoon salt
¼ teaspoon pepper

Sauce

1 (8 ounce) can tomato sauce
½ cup water
1 tablespoon vinegar

2 teaspoons dry mustard
1 tablespoon Worcestershire sauce

Combine first 7 ingredients and form into a 9x5x2½ inch loaf size and put into pan. Mix sauce ingredients, pour over meat loaf and bake at 375 degrees for 1 hour and 10 minutes.

Yield: 6 servings

Ever come nose to beak with an owl? Or hold a snake in your hands? How about turning useless kudzu vines into a beautiful basket? These are just a few of the things participants find themselves doing in our Education Department workshops. All year, our naturalists lead workshops, hikes, Discovery Programs and other activities, teaching you about our environment while you're having fun. For information about upcoming workshops, call the Callaway Gardens Education Department at (706) 663-5153.

Veal Grillades

6	(4 ounce) veal steaks (not breaded)		Flour
			Salt and pepper to taste
		1	tablespoon shortening

Sauce

½	cup coarsely chopped celery	½	cup shortening
2	large onions, coarsely chopped	6	ripe tomatoes, chopped
		1	quart beef broth
4	green peppers, coarsely chopped	2	tablespoons cornstarch
		2	tablespoons water
4	garlic cloves, minced	2	tablespoons Worcestershire sauce
2	bay leaves		

Coat veal in seasoned flour and brown on both sides in 1 tablespoon of shortening. When browned, place in a 9x13 inch glass dish. Sauté next 5 ingredients in ½ cup shortening. Add tomatoes and broth. Simmer 20 minutes. Dissolve cornstarch in water, add Worcestershire sauce, and stir into sauce mix. Cook until thickened. Pour over veal in casserole dish. Bake covered at 350 degrees for 45 minutes.

Yield: 6 servings

Veal with Mushrooms

1½	pounds veal, sliced very thin	½	pound mushrooms, sliced thin
			Salt and pepper to taste
½	teaspoon minced garlic	½	cup dry white wine
	Flour to coat veal	1	teaspoon fresh lemon juice
¼	cup butter	1	handful snipped fresh parsley

Pound veal with wooden mallet. Rub with garlic. Dip slices in flour, coating well. Heat butter in skillet until hot, add veal and sauté until golden brown on both sides. Heap thinly sliced mushrooms on veal. Sprinkle with salt (may use garlic salt or plain) and pepper, add wine. Cover skillet and cook over low heat for 20 minutes. Add water as needed to keep veal moist. Just before serving, sprinkle with lemon juice and parsley. Serve with almond rice pilaf, cooked, using chicken broth in place of water.

Yield: 6 servings

The custom designed stained-glass windows in the Ida Cason Callaway Memorial Chapel were designed by Joel Reeves, an artist from Atlanta. His design depicted scenes of nature throughout the seasons of the year. The front window depicts a Georgia hardwood forest and the back window a pine forest. The four side windows show the four seasons of the year. The windows were produced by Lloren Stained Glass Studio of Atlanta.

Tournedos au Champignons

4-6 pieces beef tenderloin, ½ inch thick
½ teaspoon salt
⅛ teaspoon pepper
1 stick butter
¼ pound fresh mushrooms, sliced
2 tablespoons chopped green onions
½ cup dry sherry
1 tablespoon brandy

Season tenderloin with salt and pepper. Heat skillet to very hot and add butter. Sauté tenderloin 2 minutes or longer on each side, according to your taste. Remove meat to a hot platter. Add mushrooms and onions to skillet, and sauté for a few minutes. Add sherry and reduce over high heat until almost dry. Add brandy and pour sauce over meat.

Worthy of a glass of red wine

Yield: 4 servings

Basil is a member of the mint family and is native to India. The minty flavor is enhanced when the herb is dried. To preserve the rich aroma, wait until the end of cooking time to add dried basil.

Pot Roast

1 (4-5 pound) pot roast
1 large onion
1 large can tomatoes, chopped
2 cups red wine
2 cups water
1 can mushroom soup
1 envelope onion soup mix
1 teaspoon basil
1 teaspoon thyme
1 medium bay leaf

Combine all in a large Dutch oven. Cover and bake for 3½ hours at 350 degrees. It is helpful to prepare a day ahead, refrigerate, slice the roast while it is cold, and then reheat in the gravy.

Yield: 8 servings

Easy London Broil Marinade

½ cup Italian dressing ½ cup steak seasoning marinade

Mix and coat each side of meat with mixture. Pierce each side well with a kitchen fork. Marinate 2-3 hours. Grill 5-10 minutes on each side, according to how well done you like your steak. Baste often. Turn often. (This works well with any cut of beef, also with pork chops or loin).

Yield: 1 cup marinade

For a tasty addition to meat and vegetable dishes, soups and sauces, bay leaves provide a woody, astringent flavor with a mild taste of mint. The leaves are most often added whole and should be removed before serving. However, to intensify the flavor, the leaf can be crumbled into the dish.

Sauce Bordelaise

2	tablespoons shallots or green onions	⅓ cup sliced fresh mushrooms
		2 tablespoons butter
¾	cup red wine	1½ tablespoons flour
½	bay leaf	1 cup strong beef broth
	Pinch thyme	Salt and pepper to taste

Finely chop shallots; add red wine, bay leaf and thyme. Simmer until wine is reduced to about ¼ cup. Strain, rubbing shallot through sieve. Sauté mushrooms in butter. Stir in flour. Add beef broth, cook and stir until mixture boils thoroughly and is clear and thickened. Add salt and pepper to taste, the wine mixture, and simmer 5 minutes.

Yield: Approximately 1¼ cups sauce to serve with filet mignon

Sauce Madère

1	finely chopped shallot or 2 small green onions	½ bay leaf
		2 teaspoons tomato paste
2	tablespoons butter	Pinch thyme
2½	tablespoons flour	Pinch pepper
1	can beef broth	3 tablespoons Madeira wine

Cook shallots (or onions) in butter until soft but not browned. Stir in flour, and cook a minute, stirring constantly. Add beef broth, bay leaf, tomato paste, thyme and pepper. Stir until mixture reaches a boil. Simmer about 5 minutes, stirring frequently. Add 3 tablespoons Madeira. Strain sauce.

Yield: Approximately 1¼ cups sauce to serve with medallions of beef

❋ *How to Cook a Country-Cured Ham*

1   (11-15 pound) ham

This is how to cook a ham, aged and cured the old-fashioned way. Soak ham overnight or wash in warm water. Put in boiler, skin side down. Cover with cold water, bring to a boil and let simmer until done, allowing 25 minutes per pound. Cool, drain and strip off skin. Sprinkle ham with brown sugar and dot with cloves. Bake at 450 degrees for 20 minutes until brown. Use a sharp knife to carve and slice very thin.

To fry ham, slice thin and trim edges. Rub skillet with ham fat and heat. Place ham in skillet and cook slowly, turning until done.

Yield: 20 servings

Country Ham 'n Red-Eye Gravy

6   slices country ham   **Black coffee**
**   Butter**

Soak ham in cold water for at least ½ hour. Wash well and dry. Fry in butter until brown. Remove from pan and keep warm. Pour black coffee into skillet with pan drippings. Stir while bringing to a boil. Serve with grits.

Yield: 6 servings

Honey Baked Ham

1   (10-12 pound) ready-to-eat   **1   cup brown sugar**
**   ham with bone**   **½   cup honey**
**   Whole cloves, as needed**   **1   teaspoon cinnamon**
3   tablespoons Dijon mustard   **1½ cups apple juice**

Score the surface of the ham in a diamond pattern, without cutting into the meat. Place a whole clove in the center of each pattern. Brush top of ham with Dijon mustard and place ham in a roasting pan. Combine sugar, honey and cinnamon; heat over medium temperature for about 3 minutes until the mixture is pourable. Spread the mixture over the ham. Pour apple juice into bottom of roasting pan and roast at 325 degrees for 1½ hours. Baste every ½ hour using the juice in the pan.

Yield: 12 servings

Dill is a member of the parsley family. The leaves, known as dillweed, have an anise-like flavor. Dill seeds are sold whole or ground and have a stronger flavor than dillweed. Dillweed can be used generously and should be added near the end of cooking time.

Glaze for Ham

1	whole ready to bake ham	4	tablespoons mustard
1	can cola-flavored carbonated beverage	1	tablespoons brown sugar Whole cloves

Preheat oven to 325 degrees. Place ham, fat side up, on rack in roasting pan; insert thermometer, being sure it does not rest in fat or on bone. Leave uncovered. Bake until thermometer reaches 160 degrees (allow 25 minutes per pound or 30 minutes per pound for ½ ham). Remove from oven about 1 hour before it is done. Remove the skin; score fat in a diamond design. Pour cola over ham. Mix mustard and sugar and spread over top of ham. Dot the diamonds with whole cloves. Return to oven for 40 to 45 minutes. Increase heat to 425 degrees and bake 15 minutes longer.

Yield: approximately 1½ cups glaze

Gingered Ham Slice

1½	pounds center cut ham, 1 inch thick	1	tablespoon salad oil
½	cup ginger ale	1½	teaspoons dry mustard
½	cup orange juice	¼	teaspoon ground ginger
¼	cup brown sugar	⅛	teaspoon ground cloves

Slash fat edge of ham. Combine all remaining ingredients. Pour over ham in a shallow glass dish. Refrigerate overnight. Spoon marinade over ham several times. Grill ham slice over low coals about 15 minutes for each side, brushing frequently with marinade. To serve, spoon a little marinade over ham.

Pineapple slices may be grilled alongside ham; brushing with sauce. Place pineapple atop ham during the last 5 to 10 minutes of grilling.

Variation of marinade: Combine ¼ cup orange juice, ¼ cup dry white wine, 1 tablespoon mustard and ¼ tablespoon ground ginger.

Yield: 4 to 6 servings

Meats, fish and even vegetables and fruit may benefit from marinating. Wet marinades contain an acid such as lemon juice, vinegar or wine plus an oil and some seasoning. A dry marinade is a blend of spices and dried herbs that is rubbed into the food. When using a wet marinade, food should be placed in a glass or stainless steel container with the marinade at least one hour. Before grilling or broiling marinated foods, drain the marinade and pat the food dry to help prevent flare-ups. To use dry marinades, wash and dry food, and lightly oil. Massage marinade rub over external surfaces of food, using one to two tablespoons of marinade per pound of food. Let stand, covered, one hour at room temperature before cooking.

Ham and Broccoli Casserole

2   (10 ounce) packages frozen
    chopped broccoli
2   cups fully cooked ham,
    chopped

1½ cups grated cheddar cheese
1   cup biscuit baking mix
3   cups milk
4   large eggs

Heat oven to 350 degrees. Cook broccoli as directed on package. Drain, spread in ungreased 13x9x2 inch baking dish. Layer ham and cheese over broccoli. Beat remaining ingredients until smooth. Slowly pour into dish over broccoli mixture. Bake uncovered, one hour at 350 degrees.

Yield: 8 servings

Ginger is grown in India, Jamaica and China. It has a characteristic pungency and is rather sweet and warm. Not only is it used in cooking, but is known to help prevent or lessen motion sickness.

Double Cooked Pork

1¼ pounds pork (preferably
    with slight fat)
1   large green pepper

3   cloves garlic
3   tablespoons cooking oil

Seasoning Sauce

2   tablespoons Hoisin sauce
1   teaspoon hot pepper sauce

1   tablespoon sugar
1   tablespoon soy sauce

Trim off outside fat. Cut meat into 2 to 3 large pieces. Simmer pork in boiling water for 25 minutes. Rinse, drain and carve into slices. Remove the seeds and membranes from the green pepper and cut into 1 inch pieces. Cut each clove of garlic into 4 to 5 lengthwise pieces. Heat 3 tablespoons oil. Stir fry pork slices for 1 minute or until meat is cooked. Add garlic and green pepper, stir fry for ½ minutes more. Remove and put aside. Use ½ tablespoon oil to cook seasoning sauce a few seconds. Return pork mixture into sauce. Coat well. Serve hot.

Use 1 tablespoon sugar, 1 tablespoon soy sauce and 1 teaspoon brown gravy syrup as a substitute for Hoisin sauce.

Yield: 6 servings

Roast Pork with Herbs

5	pounds pork loin		Pepper and nutmeg
	Salt and rosemary	1	cup thinly sliced onions
	Oregano, thyme and sage	1	cup thinly sliced carrots

Sautéed sweet peppers

½	cup olive oil	6-7	green and red peppers
1	cup sliced onions		(2 pounds)
1	clove garlic, crushed	1	teaspoon salt
		⅛	teaspoon pepper

Herb gravy

¼	cup pan drippings	Boiling water
¼	cup unsifted all-purpose flour	

Preheat oven to 325 degrees. Wipe pork with damp paper towels. Combine 2 teaspoons each salt and rosemary; 1½ teaspoons each oregano, thyme and sage; ¼ teaspoon each pepper and nutmeg. With a sharp knife, make ½ inch deep slits in fat between the ribs. Press half of herb mixture into slits; rub the rest of the herbs on surface of meat. Insert meat thermometer in center of roast, away from bone. Place roast, fat side up, in a shallow roasting pan without rack. Scatter onions and carrots around roast. Roast 3 hours, or until thermometer registers 185 degrees. Sautéed Sweet Peppers: Wash peppers. Slice into ¾ inch wide strips; remove ribs and seeds. In hot oil in large skillet, sauté onion and garlic 5 minutes, stirring occasionally. Add the peppers and sauté 10 minutes, stirring occasionally. Sprinkle with salt and pepper. Remove roast to heated platter; surround with peppers; keep warm in low oven. To prepare gravy, strain pan drippings, reserve ¼ cup, discard onion and carrot. In saucepan, mix reserved drippings and flour until smooth. Pour 2¾ cups boiling water into roasting pan. Return to boiling, stir to loosen and dissolve brown particles in pan. Continue boiling, stirring about 2 minutes. Slowly pour boiling liquid into the flour mixture, stirring briskly with a wire whisk to avoid lumps. Add ½ teaspoon salt, ¼ teaspoon rosemary, ⅛ teaspoon each oregano, thyme, sage and pepper, and a dash of nutmeg. Bring to boiling, stirring. Reduce heat; simmer, covered, 5 minutes. Stir, serve with roast.

Yield: 8 servings

Hot Barbecue Ribs

4   pounds pork ribs

Sauce

¼   cup molasses
¼   cup prepared mustard
¼   cup lemon juice

1   tablespoon Worcestershire
     sauce
½   teaspoon hot pepper sauce
¼   teaspoon salt

Simmer ribs in salted water 45 to 60 minutes, until tender. While ribs are simmering, make sauce by mixing all ingredients and heat to boiling. Grill ribs 10 to 15 minutes on each side, brushing often with sauce.

Yield: 4 servings

Chicken Breasts Supreme

**6   whole chicken breasts,
      halved**

Marinade

1   cup sour cream
¼   cup lemon juice
4   teaspoons Worcestershire
     sauce
1½ teaspoons celery salt

2   teaspoons paprika
1   teaspoon garlic powder
1½ teaspoons salt
½   teaspoon black pepper

Topping

½   cup margarine
½   cup shortening

1¼ cups bread crumbs

Wash and wipe chicken breasts with paper towel. In a large glass or ceramic bowl, combine sour cream with the next 7 ingredients. Add chicken breasts to the marinade, coating well. Let stand, covered, overnight in refrigerator. Next day, remove chicken from marinade and roll in bread crumbs, coating well. Arrange in single layer in a large shallow pan. At this point, you may freeze for later use. Preheat oven to 350 degrees. Topping: Melt shortening and margarine, mixing together with bread crumbs. Spoon half of mixture over chicken. Bake, covered for 1 hour. Spoon rest of butter mixture over chicken and bake uncovered for 15 minutes longer.

Yield: 12 servings

Bright red paprika adds color and a mild sweet pepper flavor to many dishes. It is sold ground and is best preserved by keeping refrigerated.

Chicken Sauternes

8	boneless chicken breast halves	1	tablespoon all-purpose flour
	Salt, garlic-pepper and paprika, to taste	1	cup water
		8	ounces fresh mushrooms, chopped
1	stick butter or margarine	¾	cup Sauterne wine
1	medium onion, chopped		

Preheat oven to 350 degrees. Generously sprinkle chicken breasts with seasonings. In a large skillet, melt the butter over medium to high heat and brown chicken breasts lightly on both sides. Remove chicken from skillet and place in a 9x13x2 inch baking dish. To the skillet, add the onions and cook over medium heat until transparent. Add flour and stir to combine. Slowly add water, stirring constantly, to make a smooth sauce. Add mushrooms, and wine. Pour over chicken breasts. Bake for 30 minutes or until chicken is done.

This dish is better if made the day before and refrigerated. When ready to serve, bring to room temperature before reheating.

Yield: 8 servings

Chicken Divan

2	(10 ounce) packages chopped broccoli	1	teaspoon lemon juice
2	cups cooked chicken, diced	½	teaspoon curry powder
2	(10¾ ounce) cans cream of chicken soup	½	cup shredded cheddar cheese
1	cup mayonnaise	½	cup bread crumbs, buttered

Cook broccoli until tender, drain and arrange in greased 11½x7½x 1½ inch baking dish. Place chicken on top. Combine soup, mayonnaise, lemon juice and curry powder; pour over chicken. Sprinkle with cheese and bread crumbs. Bake at 350 degrees for 25 to 30 minutes.

Yield: 8 servings

Daisy Bonner's Country Captain

1	hen or 2 fryers	½	cup currants or raisins, divided
2	green peppers, chopped		
1	garlic clove, minced	1	teaspoon thyme
2	onions, chopped	1	teaspoon curry powder
1	large can tomatoes		Salt and pepper to taste
1	(4 ounce) can mushrooms	2	cups rice, boiled until dry
½	cup almonds or other nuts, divided		

Boil chickens until tender. Debone. Mix green pepper, onions, tomatoes, mushrooms, ¼ cup nuts, ¼ cup currants, thyme, curry powder, salt and pepper. Add chicken. Simmer for one hour. (Can be simmered on stove or in casserole dish in oven.) Serve over rice. Garnish with chopped green peppers, currants and nuts. Sauce should be thin.

Yield: 12 servings

Daisy Bonner was President Franklin D. Roosevelt's cook whenever he was in residence at the Little White House in Warm Springs. She always served baked grapefruit, French beans, plain salad, rolls, chocolate soufflé and coffee with this dish.

Chicken with Dried Beef

3	(5 ounce) jars chipped beef	2	(10¾ ounce) cans cream of chicken soup
10	boneless chicken breasts		
10	strips bacon	¼	cup dry Vermouth
1	pound fresh mushrooms, sliced		

Arrange chipped beef in 9x13 inch casserole dish. Wrap bacon around each breast and place on top of beef with bacon seam down. Distribute sliced mushrooms evenly on top of chicken. Mix soup and Vermouth and pour over all. Cover with foil. Bake for 2 hours at 300 degrees then for 30 minutes at 350 degrees. Keep foil in place the entire baking time.

Yield: 10 servings

Ida's Chicken Casserole

1	onion, chopped	1	large hen roasted or boiled and deboned
1	stick butter or margarine		
2	cups chicken stock	1	(16 ounce) bag spinach noodles, cooked
2	(10¾ ounce) cans cream of mushroom soup		
		1	(3 ounce) jar chopped green olives
1	pound pasteurized process cheese loaf		
			Cracker crumbs

Sauté the onion in the butter. Add chicken stock and mushroom soup. Add Velveeta. Combine chicken, noodles, and the cheese sauce. Add green olives. Pour into a buttered 9x13 inch casserole dish. Sprinkle with cracker crumbs and bake at 350 degrees for 30 minutes.

Yield: 6 servings

Fireworks over Robin Lake are the traditional culmination to the festive July 4th Surf and Sand celebration at Robin Lake Beach. The day begins early and ends late and is filled with entertainment, "Flying High" circus performances, swimming, beach games, picnicking and more. As the darkness falls, the sky lights up with spectacular explosions of color to make this a day to remember.

Loaded with Calories Chicken Bake

1	(8 ounce) package bread stuffing mix	1	(8 ounce) package fresh mushrooms, sliced
1	stick butter or margarine	1	(16 ounce) carton sour cream
6	chicken breasts, boned and cooked		Salt and pepper to taste
1	medium onion, sliced thinly	2	cups very sharp cheddar cheese, grated
½	cup milk		
1	(10¾ ounce) can cream of mushroom soup		

Sprinkle dry stuffing mix in a large 13x9x2 inch baking pan. Dot with butter. Place chicken breasts on top; put sliced onion on chicken. Mix milk with soup (will be thick). Spoon over chicken and onions. Spread sliced mushrooms over soup mixture. Dollop all of sour cream over mushrooms. Dot with remaining butter. Add salt and pepper. Bake at 350 degrees for 1 hour. Cover with cheese and broil until cheese is brown.

Yield: 6 servings

My Favorite Chicken

8	chicken breasts, skinned, deboned	4	slices bacon
8	ounces sharp cheddar cheese, sliced	8	ounces sour cream
1	jar dried beef	1	(10¾ ounce) can mushroom soup

Pound chicken breasts until slightly flat. Roll each one around a piece of cheese (about one ounce). Place a piece of dried beef around chicken breast, then a piece of bacon and secure with a toothpick. Marinate overnight in a mixture of sour cream and mushroom soup. Bake covered at 350 degrees for 1½ hours. Uncover the last few minutes and let brown slightly.

Marinate in a baking dish covered with foil and bake in same dish.

Yield: 8 servings

One Pot Chicken and Rice Bake

	Olive oil	1	large red pepper, sliced
1	(14 ounce) box long grain brown rice	1	pound okra, sliced
6	whole chicken breasts	3	garlic cloves, minced
	Salt and pepper to taste	4	cups chicken broth
1	large onion, sliced	3	tablespoons fresh chopped parsley
½	pound mushrooms, sliced		

In large roaster, drizzle olive oil to thinly cover bottom of pan. Sprinkle box of rice over bottom of pan. Season chicken with salt and pepper and brown in olive oil in a large frying pan. Remove chicken and place in roaster on top of rice. In same frying pan, brown onion, mushrooms, red pepper, okra and garlic in olive oil. This may need to be done in 2 or 3 batches depending on size of frying pan. Remove vegetables to roaster on top of chicken. Pour chicken stock over all. Sprinkle with parsley. Bake at 400 degrees for 45 minutes.

Yield: 6 servings

Each January, gardening experts and amateurs meet at Callaway Gardens for the Southern Gardening Symposium to discuss and learn about gardening in the South. This three-day annual event provides a wealth of ideas and information to make even the most experienced gardener improve his expertise.

❋ Oriental Chicken

½	cup butter	2	cups chicken, cooked and diced
½	cup flour	½	cup mushrooms, sautéed
1	tablespoon salt	½	cup almonds, blanched
1	cup cream or evaporated milk	1	cup sliced water chestnuts
3	cups milk	¼	cup pimento, cut in strips
2	cups chicken stock	¼	cup sherry

Melt butter in top of double boiler, add flour and salt and cook until bubbly; add cream, milk and chicken stock, stirring until smooth. Cook over hot water for 30 minutes. Just before serving, add and heat thoroughly; the chicken, mushrooms, almonds, water chestnuts, pimento and sherry. Serve over cheese soufflé, in a pastry shell, over rice, or whatever you please, but over soufflé is most delightful!

A truly elegant entrée. You may reserve the mushrooms, sauté them whole and top each serving with one. Fresh asparagus served across a grilled tomato completes a beautiful plate. This freezes beautifully.

Yield: 8 to 10 servings

Smothered Chicken

1	(3 pound) young chicken	½	teaspoon salt
4	tablespoons butter	1	pint milk
2	tablespoons flour		

Wash, draw and split chicken down the back. Chicken may be cut up same as for frying. Wipe dry inside and out. Sprinkle with salt and pepper and place flat in a greased baking dish. Make a sauce of the butter, flour, salt and milk. Pour over the chicken. Bake at 350 degrees for 1½ hours or until chicken is tender and lightly browned. Garnish with parsley and serve in the baking dish.

If gravy has curdled during cooking, remove chicken and add a little blended milk and flour. Stir until smooth and return the chicken and reheat.

Yield: 6 servings

Get out your needle and thread and head for the Callaway School of Needlearts. Two one-week sessions of the school are devoted to classes in every type of needlework imaginable. In addition to classes, participants enjoy meals, accommodations, a banquet and a marketplace. A juried competition is open to the public. Needleartists from across the country participate in the Callaway School of Needlearts.

Pecan Crusted Chicken Breasts

6   skinless boneless chicken
    breasts

Marinade

3	tablespoons sesame oil	1	tablespoon lemon juice
2	tablespoons vegetable oil	1	tablespoon soy sauce
2	tablespoons minced onion	1	tablespoon hot water
1	teaspoon grated lemon rind		

Coating

1	cup crushed stoned wheat crackers	2	tablespoons fresh parsley
½	cup Parmesan cheese	½	teaspoon black pepper
¼	cup chopped fresh basil	½	cup toasted pecan pieces

Topping

4   tablespoons unsalted butter,
    melted

Wash and pat dry the chicken breasts. Place chicken in a large ziplock bag or glass or ceramic bowl. Combine marinade ingredients and pour over chicken. Let stand in refrigerator up to 2 hours. Preheat oven to 350 degrees. Combine coating ingredients in a food processor or blender and process to crumbs. Remove chicken breasts from the marinade; discard marinade. Coat both sides of breasts with the processed crumbs. Place in a buttered baking dish. Drizzle with 4 tablespoons melted unsalted butter. Bake in 350 degree oven for 45 minutes or until cooked through.

Yield: 6 servings

The John A. Sibley Horticultural Center features an indoor 22-foot waterfall. Each minute 350 gallons spill into a pool below. Visitors may walk safely under the waterfall to enjoy the coolness of a stone grotto. Many visitors toss coins into the grotto. Legend is that if the coin catches on a stone, your wish will come true.

Polynesian Delight

1½ pounds breaded chicken breast fillets or chicken fingers	1 (24 ounce) jar prepared sweet and sour sauce for chicken
½ cup artichoke hearts	1 (15¼ ounce) chunk pineapple, drain and reserve juice
1 cup chopped celery	
1 cup chopped onion	
1 cup chopped bell pepper	1 (11 ounce) can Mandarin oranges, drain and reserve juice
10 mushroom caps, sliced	
2 tablespoons olive oil	
2 teaspoons minced garlic	3 teaspoons cornstarch
1 (16 ounce) package frozen stir fry vegetables	1 dash soy sauce
	Rice

Layer chicken in bottom of large roaster or pan. Sauté raw, chopped vegetables in olive oil, add minced garlic and the package of stir fry vegetables. Continue to sauté. Then add sweet and sour sauce, pineapple, and oranges, mixing well. Mix cornstarch with reserved fruit juices to thicken. Pour all vegetable mixture over chicken, dribble thickened sauce over all. Add a little soy sauce. Bake in 350 degree oven for 30 to 45 minutes. Serve over rice.

Yield: 6 servings

Stewed Chicken and Cabbage

1 chicken, cut into serving pieces	1 medium ripe tomato, peeled and sliced
1½ tablespoons lemon juice	3 teaspoons salad oil
Salt and pepper to taste	1 clove garlic, crushed
1 scallion, chopped	2 teaspoons sugar
1 medium onion, sliced	1 small cabbage, sliced

Place chicken pieces in a large bowl. Sprinkle lemon juice, salt and pepper onto chicken, add scallion, onion and tomato. Mix thoroughly. Allow to marinate 15 to 30 minutes. Heat oil in skillet and brown garlic. Remove garlic and discard. Add sugar and heat until dark brown. Add chicken (putting marinade aside) and brown on all sides over medium heat. Add marinated mixture and allow to cook for two minutes uncovered. Cover and cook for ten minutes, remove chicken. Add cabbage and cook for five minutes more. Serve over rice, noodles, spaghetti or potatoes.

Yield: 8 servings

The John A. Sibley Horticultural Center is an indoor/outdoor display garden and greenhouse. Twenty-six folding glass doors that are 24-feet tall and weigh 1,600 pounds each can be easily opened during warm weather so that the indoor and outdoor gardens may flow together.

Turkey Gumbo

1	turkey carcass	½	teaspoon thyme
4	tablespoons flour	1	cup sausage, smoked and sliced
4	tablespoons bacon drippings		
1	cup chopped green onions	3	cups turkey meat
1	cup chopped celery		Salt and pepper to taste
4	tablespoons chopped parsley	1	pint oysters and liquid
		1	tablespoon gumbo filé
3	bay leaves	2	cups cooked rice

Cook turkey carcass with at least 8 cups of water. Boil 1 hour or until meat falls off bone. Strain and reserve 6 cups of turkey broth. Make roux by combining the bacon drippings and flour in a large Dutch oven. Cook over low heat, stirring constantly until roux is a caramel color (15 to 20 minutes). Stir in onions, celery, parsley and sauté 3 minutes. Add broth and all other ingredients (except oysters, filé and rice) and cook over low heat for 1½ to 2 hours. Do not boil. Add oysters and gumbo filé at end. Serve over hot cooked rice.

Yield: 6 servings

Benjamin Franklin proposed that the turkey be our national bird, rather than the bald eagle.

Williamsburg Chicken

4	cups diced chicken	3	tablespoons minced onion, fresh or dried
2	cups diced celery		
1	(8 ounce) can water chestnuts, diced and drained	1	(10¾ ounce) can cream of chicken soup
4	large boiled eggs, diced	1	(10¾ ounce) can cream of mushroom or celery soup
¾	cup mayonnaise		

Mix all ingredients well. Place in casserole dish. Bake at 350 degrees for 30 to 40 minutes. Top this with crushed snack crackers and drizzle with butter, if desired.

Yield: 8 servings

Delicious Smothered Baked Quail

4	quail		Salt and pepper to taste
1	package dry onion soup mix	4	strips bacon

Place quail into deep baking pan with lid. Sprinkle dry onion soup mix on top. Add salt and pepper. Place bacon on top and cover. Bake at 275 degrees for 3 to 4 hours.

Substitute 1 stick melted margarine for the soup mix and bacon. Salt and pepper quail, dip in margarine, roll in flour. Place in baking pan and pour any remaining margarine on top. Cover with foil and bake at 350 degrees for 1 hour.

Yield: 4 servings

The Sibley Horticultural Center is named after John A. Sibley (1888-1986), a close family friend of the Callaways. Sibley was president and chairman of the board of directors of the Trust Company of Georgia. He shared the Callaways concern for proper land use and conservation.

❋ Quail and Chipped Beef

6	quail	2	cups milk
1	(2½ ounce) jar dried beef	½	cup quail broth
3	tablespoons butter	½	teaspoon salt
3	tablespoons flour		Pepper

Parboil quail. When cool, remove meat from bones. Boil down the quail broth. Remove dried beef from jar and shred. Soak in fresh boiling water a few minutes. Melt butter and stir in flour. When bubbly, add milk slowly and cook, stirring constantly, until thick. Add about ½ cup of quail broth. Add ½ teaspoon salt and a dash of pepper. Add chipped beef and quail. Recipe may be easily doubled. Serve on baked, sliced cornbread that has been buttered and toasted.

Chicken may be substituted for quail.

Yield: 6 servings

Country Fried Quail

12	quail	¼	cup milk
	Salt and pepper to taste		Flour
2	large eggs, well beaten	1	quart oil

Cut quail in half and sprinkle with salt and pepper. Make batter of milk and eggs. Dip quail in batter, then in flour. Fry in hot oil; browning on both sides. Serve hot.

Yield: 12 servings

Quail in Wine

8	quail	1	tablespoon flour
	Salt and pepper	1	cup chicken broth (canned)
1	stick margarine	¾	cup dry white wine
1	medium onion, finely chopped	1	(8 ounce) package fresh sliced mushrooms

Salt and pepper quail. Brown carefully (not too high heat) in heavy skillet (iron preferably) in the margarine. Remove to 9x13 inch baking dish. Sauté onion in drippings. Stir in flour, broth and wine. Pour over quail. Cover and bake at 275 degrees for 1½ hours. Turn quail every 30 minutes. Add mushrooms on last turn. If more gravy is desired, add more broth and flour. This recipe doubles and triples easily. Serve with wild rice.

Use red wine in place of white, and add ½ cup tomato sauce. Sauté ½ cup each green pepper and celery along with the onion.

Yield: 8 servings

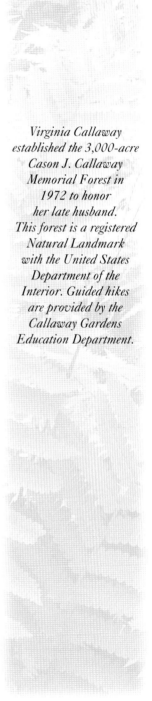

Virginia Callaway established the 3,000-acre Cason J. Callaway Memorial Forest in 1972 to honor her late husband. This forest is a registered Natural Landmark with the United States Department of the Interior. Guided hikes are provided by the Callaway Gardens Education Department.

Wild Turkey, Dressing and Giblet Gravy

Wild Turkey

1 (12-14 pound) wild turkey	½ cup butter
Salt	¼ cup flour

Remove neck and giblets and reserve for giblet gravy. Rinse bird thoroughly inside and out with cold water; pat dry. Sprinkle entire surface of bird lightly with salt and rub breast, drumsticks and wings with ½ cup butter until creamy; then pat with ¼ cup flour. Stuff neck cavity with small amount of dressing, fasten skin to back with skewer; lightly stuff large cavity. Tie drumsticks together or tuck under band of skin at tail if this has been left on. Fold wing tips across the back of bird. Place bird on roasting rack in drip pan, breast side up. Insert meat thermometer in breast or thickest part of drumstick, making sure it does not touch the bone. Bake at 325 degrees for 1 hour or until bird begins to brown. Reduce heat to 300 degrees and bake for 20 minutes per pound (about 4 to 5 hours) or until thermometer reaches 185 degrees. Bird will be very brown. Rotate pan one half turn every 20 minutes and baste with drippings the entire baking time. When bird is two-thirds done, open cavity and spread drumsticks; this will permit the inside of the thighs to be cooked sufficiently. The bird is done when the thermometer reaches 185 degrees or when drumsticks can be moved up and down easily. Remove from oven and let cool for 20 minutes before carving.

Dressing

¾ cup finely chopped shallots or onions	1 tablespoon sage
1½ cups finely chopped celery	¼ teaspoon allspice
½ cup finely chopped parsley	12 cups soft bread crumbs
1 cup butter, melted	2 cups boiled peanuts, hulled
½ teaspoon pepper	1 tablespoon salt
½ teaspoon marjoram	4½ cups water

Sauté onions, celery and parsley in butter until tender. Add remaining ingredients. Mix well. Spoon into turkey cavities. Spoon remaining dressing into greased baking dish and bake at 350 degrees for 45 minutes to 1 hour until lightly browned. This recipe may be cut in half for use with smaller birds.

Wild Turkey, Dressing and Giblet Gravy (continued)

Giblet Gravy

3	cups water	6	tablespoons all-purpose
1	teaspoon salt		flour
	Neck and giblets from wild		Water
	turkey		Salt and pepper to taste

Combine 3 cups water and 1 teaspoon salt in medium saucepan. Bring to a boil. Reduce heat; add neck and giblets and simmer 15 minutes. Remove liver and continue simmering remaining giblets until tender. Remove giblets from broth; discard neck; chop meat and return to broth. Blend flour and small amounts of water into smooth paste; stir into broth. Cook, stirring constantly, until desired thickness is attained. Add salt and pepper to taste.

Yield: 12 servings

Deer Roast (Hind Quarter)

1	hind quarter deer, deboned		Salt and pepper to taste

Marinade

1	large onion, sliced	2	cups Spanish barbecue sauce
5	cloves garlic		Salt and pepper to taste
3	bay leaves	8	bacon strips
2	tablespoons oregano	1	turkey size cooking bag

Debone hind quarter and make cuts in meat with knife. Salt and pepper to taste. Add all ingredients and cover with bacon strips. Marinate in cooking bag for 5 hours. Cook according to weight as directed on cooking bag. Scrumptious!

Spanish barbecue sauce can be found in Spanish section of supermarket.

Yield: 10 servings

American Indians extensively used wild turkeys as a source of food and feathers. Certain tribes, however, considered turkeys stupid and cowardly and did not eat them for fear of acquiring these traits!

Southern Quail

4	quail	¼	cup dry sherry
4	celery ribs	½	cup dry vermouth
8	slices carrots	½	cup chicken stock
2	tablespoons butter		Salt and pepper
2	tablespoons olive oil	1	pinch oregano
1	onion, sliced	2	tablespoons chopped
6	ripe black olives		parsley
1	cup white wine		

Insert in cavity of each quail: 1 rib celery and 2 slices of carrot. Sauté quail in butter and olive oil until lightly browned. Add onion to pan and sauté lightly. Add olives, wines, stock, salt, pepper and oregano. Cover and cook slowly until quail are tender, about 1 hour. Just before serving, add parsley.

Yield: 4 servings

Smothered Doves

12	doves	1	teaspoon prepared mustard
	Salt and pepper to taste		Juice of 2 lemons
2½	sticks butter, melted	1	cup hot water
3	tablespoons		
	Worcestershire sauce		

Sprinkle birds with salt and pepper. Brown in butter. Combine Worcestershire sauce, mustard, and lemon juice. Pour mixture over browned birds. Add 1 cup hot water. Cover and cook on low heat for 1½ hours, basting often. Add more water if necessary, but never let water cover the birds.

Yield: 12 servings

Steak à la Milonesa

6   breaded venison steaks

Sauce

½   cup olive oil
1   medium onion, sliced
4   garlic cloves, sliced
1   green pepper, sliced
2   (8 ounce) cans tomato sauce

½   can water
4   hard-boiled eggs, diced
1   (15¼ ounce) can green
     peas, drained

Fry breaded steaks, browning on both sides. Put into 9x13 inch baking dish. Put olive oil in saucepan; add onion, garlic and green pepper. Cook for about 10 minutes; add tomato sauce and water. Cook for 10 more minutes. Pour sauce over cooked steaks. Bake in 325 degree oven for 1 hour. Serve with rice or noodles. Garnish with diced eggs and peas.

Yield: 6 servings

"Most of the good things civilization has achieved are the result of somebody seeing, in his mind's eye, how to do something better or make something better."
— Cason Callaway

Venison Steak

¼   cup Worcestershire sauce
1   teaspoon salt
1   teaspoon pepper
1   teaspoon powdered ginger
1   tablespoon chopped garlic

1   pound venison steak, sliced
     and tenderized
Flour
Vegetable or olive oil

Mix first 5 ingredients. Marinate venison steak in sauce for 2 to 3 hours in the refrigerator. Roll slices in flour. Brown on both sides in vegetable or olive oil until done.

Yield: 4 servings

Venison Chili

1	pound ground venison	1	green bell pepper, diced
1	pound ground beef	4	(10¾ ounce) cans tomato
4	cloves garlic, diced		soup
1	teaspoon oregano	4	cans water
2	bay leaves	1	teaspoon chili powder
	Salt and pepper to taste	2	(16 ounce) cans red kidney
1	large onion, diced		beans
1	(8 ounce) can tomato		Hot peppers to taste
	sauce		(optional)
1	tablespoon chili powder		

Brown venison and ground meat together. Add garlic, oregano, bay leaves, salt, pepper, onion, tomato sauce, chili powder and green pepper and set aside. In a large pot, cook tomato soup, water and chili powder on high for 20 minutes. Drain grease from browned meat and add to mixture. Add kidney beans and cook for 30 minutes. Serve with grated cheese and onions or over rice.

Yield: 10 servings

Scallops Amelia

¼	cup chopped green onions	1	teaspoon cornstarch
½	teaspoon minced garlic	2	tablespoons white wine
3	tablespoons butter	½	cup halved seedless green
1	pound sea scallops, rinsed		grapes (optional)
1	cup fresh mushrooms,		Bread crumbs
	sliced		

Sauté green onions in butter with garlic for 1 minute. Add scallops and mushrooms. Simmer covered for 5 minutes. Blend cornstarch and wine until smooth. Add to scallops; cook 1 minute. Grapes can be added at this time. Remove to baking dishes or shells. Sprinkle with bread crumbs. Broil on top oven shelf until brown.

Yield: 4 servings

Baked Fish Fillets in Lime Juice and Sour Cream

2	pounds fish fillets	1	cup sour cream
	Salt and pepper to taste	¼	teaspoon parsley
1	large lime		

Place fish fillets in 9x13 inch baking dish. Salt and pepper to taste. Squeeze juice from lime and grate peeling. Mix together lime juice, sour cream, parsley, dash of salt and pepper. Pour sour cream mixture over fish and sprinkle top with grated lime peel. Bake at 350 degrees for 30 minutes.

Yield: 6 servings

Fried Oysters

1	quart oysters, select	½	teaspoon pepper
2	eggs beaten well	1	cup cracker meal or yellow
2	tablespoons milk		cornmeal
1	teaspoon salt		

Drain oysters and lay on paper towels. Beat eggs and add milk. Season with salt and pepper. Dip oysters into mixture and gently roll in meal. Fry in hot cooking oil, turning only once. Remove when golden. Do not overcook. Drain on paper towels.

Yield: 8 servings

Oyster Stew

4	tablespoons butter	4	cups milk
1	teaspoon Worcestershire	1½	teaspoons salt
	sauce		Pepper to taste
1	pint raw oysters, well drained		

Melt butter over low heat in saucepan. Add Worcestershire sauce and oysters. Heat until edge of oysters begin to curl. Add milk, salt and pepper. Heat well, but do not boil. Serve with oyster crackers.

In order to avoid overcooking, heat the milk in one pot and pour over the oysters.

Yield: 6 servings

Although there is no business connection among them, the founders/owners of Callaway Gardens, Callaway Golf, Callaway Corvettes, Callaway Editions, Callaway Winery and The Callaway Racing Team are all family related but different companies.

Salmon Croquettes

1	(14¾ ounce) can pink or red salmon, drained	1	tablespoon lemon juice
⅓	cup self-rising cornmeal	½	teaspoon black pepper
¼	cup all-purpose flour	½	cup buttermilk with pinch of baking soda stirred in
1	large egg, beaten		

Mix all ingredients well. Shape into flat patties. Fry in hot oil until brown on both sides. Drain on paper towels.

Yield: 8 servings

Wildlife is abundant around Callaway Gardens — including approximately 50 kinds of mammals; 200 bird species; 35 kinds of snakes; eight types of lizards; a dozen turtle species; and two dozen kinds of frogs, toads and salamanders.

Salmon Mousse with Cucumber Sauce

Mousse

1	tablespoon plain gelatin	1	teaspoon dried dill weed
2	tablespoons fresh lemon juice	½	teaspoon paprika
1	small onion sliced	1	(14¾ ounce) can red salmon
½	cup cold water	1	cup whipping cream
½	cup mayonnaise		

Cucumber Sauce

1	pint sour cream	½	teaspoon cayenne pepper
3	tablespoons white wine vinegar	2	teaspoons grated onion
1	tablespoon fresh lemon juice	3	tablespoons dill weed
1	teaspoon salt	1	cup cucumber, peeled, seeded and diced

Put gelatin, lemon juice, onion and water in blender; purée. Add mayonnaise, dill weed, paprika and salmon; blend well. Add cream gradually, blend for a few seconds. Pour into oiled 4 cup mold. Chill until set. (A fish mold is nice.) Prepare sauce by placing all ingredients in blender and whirl until smooth. Serve with Mousse.

Yield: 8 servings

Marinade for Shrimp

1	cup Wesson vegetable oil	1	teaspoon ground red pepper
½	cup vinegar	1	tablespoon salt
¼	cup Worcestershire sauce		Handful bay leaves
1	tablespoon paprika	1	medium onion, sliced and
2	tablespoons hot sauce		separated into rings

Combine all ingredients. Heat sauce to almost boiling and pour over peeled, cooked shrimp. It is best to layer shrimp with bay leaves and onion rings.

This recipe originated with a chef at the old Houston Hotel in Dothan, Alabama. The onion rings are as good as the shrimp!

Yield: 1¾ cups

There are more than 2,000 species of shrimp and, contrary to popular belief, there is no difference between prawns and shrimp.

Seafood Chowder

2	medium onions, diced	1	(28 ounce) can tomatoes
6	cloves garlic, diced	2	quarts hot water
1	large green pepper, diced	1	teaspoon Worcestershire
5	bay leaves		sauce
1	tablespoon oregano	½	teaspoon black pepper
½	cup olive oil	2	teaspoons salt
1	(6 ounce) can tomato paste	6	cups seafood, cut up

Fry onions, garlic, green pepper, bay leaves and oregano in olive oil. When done, add tomato paste, tomatoes and water. Add remaining ingredients and seafood. Simmer uncovered approximately 2 hours. Serve with hot bread or crackers.

Crabmeat, lobster, shrimp, scallops are a good mixture of seafood. Other combinations, fresh or canned, may be substituted.

A hot pepper may be added while simmering.

Yield: 8 to 10 servings

Shrimp and Grits

1 cup bacon, chopped	1 pound shrimp
½ cup sliced green pepper	2 tablespoons hot pepper
½ cup sliced sweet red pepper	sauce

Grits

1 cup chicken broth	¼ teaspoon salt
1½ cups milk	1 cup shredded cheddar
¾ cup speckled heart grits	cheese

Cook bacon in skillet until crisp. Remove, drain and set aside. Sauté peppers in 2 tablespoons of reserved bacon drippings; remove from skillet and set aside. Sauté shrimp in skillet until pink; return peppers, add hot sauce and serve over grits. Prepare grits by bringing broth and milk to boil. Add grits and salt. Return to a boil; reduce heat to medium, cover and cook for about 20 to 30 minutes, stirring often to prevent sticking. Add cheese and stir to melt.

Yield: 4 servings

Shrimp Curry

5 pounds raw shrimp	4 tablespoons curry powder
Juice of 2 lemons	½ teaspoon powdered ginger
2 cups chicken broth	4 teaspoons salt
10 tablespoons butter	3 teaspoons sugar
1 cup minced onion	1 quart milk
12 tablespoons flour	Minced parsley

Clean and cook shrimp. Toss with lemon juice and refrigerate. (Drain and save juice for adding to sauce.) Cook onion in melted butter. With slotted spoon remove onions and reserve. Use butter to make sauce with flour, curry, ginger, salt, sugar, broth and milk. Blend in blender. Return to stove and cook in double boiler over hot water until thickened. Mix with onion, shrimp and lemon juice. Refrigerate overnight. Reheat and serve with, or on, 10 to 12 cups of hot cooked rice which has been tossed with 2 tablespoons minced parsley. Serve with side dishes of chutney, shredded coconut, chopped peanuts or pickle relish.

Use part coconut milk for the quart of milk.

Yield: 12 servings

Key West Fried Shrimp

1	pound shrimp, deveined			Garlic powder to taste
3	tablespoons lime or lemon juice		1	egg
	Salt and pepper to taste		½	cup milk
			1	box cracker meal

Mix lime juice, salt, pepper and garlic and marinate shrimp at least one hour. Mix egg with milk and add salt, pepper and garlic powder. Dip shrimp in this mixture, then in cracker meal. Pat down to coat all over. Use enough oil to deep fry. Heat oil until a haze begins to rise. Put shrimp in a few at a time, to prevent sudden cooling of oil temperature. Fry until brown all over, drain on paper.

After draining, if you will place shrimp in a brown grocery bag and place it in a low oven until all shrimp are cooked, shrimp will not get soggy. Do not cover.

Recipe may also be used for fish.

Yield: 4 servings

Grilled Rosemary Shrimp

3	pounds large shrimp, unpeeled		½	cup olive oil
1	bunch fresh rosemary crushed			Juice of 2 lemons and 1 lemon, sliced
6	garlic cloves, minced			Salt and pepper to taste

To prepare shrimp, use a small knife, cut a slit lengthwise along inner curve of each shrimp. Insert 2 to 3 sprigs rosemary leaves into slit. In a large bowl, whisk together garlic, oil, lemon juice, salt and pepper, to taste. Toss shrimp in oil mixture, coating well. Add more rosemary sprigs and lemon slices. Cover and refrigerate 1 to 2 hours. Drain shrimp and grill on skewers or use grill basket over medium heat 5 minutes on each side or until shrimp are opaque.

Yield: 6 servings

Approximately half of the butterflies in the Day Butterfly Center come from the Center's production house. The other portion come from various butterfly farmers abroad.

Garlic Buttered Shrimp

¼	cup butter	1	dash cayenne
1	clove garlic, minced	3	tablespoons dry white wine
1	tablespoon parsley snipped	1	pound shrimp, shelled and
1	teaspoon all-purpose		deveined or frozen jumbo
	seasoning		

In saucepan, melt butter. Stir in garlic, parsley, all-purpose seasoning and cayenne, cook 1 to 2 minutes. Stir in wine; heat through. Thaw frozen shrimp. Thread shrimp on small skewers. Grill over medium-hot coals about 7 minutes. Turn frequently and brush with sauce.

Yield: 15 to 18 appetizers

The birdstudy area in the courtyard of the Callaway Gardens Inn is named after Athos Menaboni, an Italian artist famous for his wildlife paintings. Menaboni was a close friend of Cason and Virginia Callaway. Many of his paintings and sculptures are on display at Callaway Gardens.

Georgia Mountain Trout in Wine

6	pieces trout	2	medium onions thinly sliced
	Salt and pepper to taste	½	cup chopped parsley
	Juice of 2 fresh lemons	½	cup dry white wine
3	large tomatoes sliced and	¼	cup chicken bouillon
	peeled		

Oil shallow baking dish, place the trout seasoned with salt and pepper (sprinkle outside and rub inside cavity), and lemon juice. Cover trout with sliced tomatoes; then cover tomatoes with sliced onions. Sprinkle with chopped parsley. Pour wine and chicken bouillon over all. Bake uncovered 30 minutes at 400 degrees. Garnish with lemon slices and parsley. Serve with brown rice.

Yield: 6 servings

Georgia Garden Paella

¼	cup olive oil	2	dashes Worcestershire sauce
2	medium onions, chopped	½	teaspoon saffron, crushed
1	bell pepper, chopped		Salt and pepper to taste
2-3	ribs celery	½	pound broccoli, chopped
3-4	cloves garlic	1	zucchini, chopped
1	tablespoon oregano	1	choyte squash, chopped
2-3	bay leaves	1	medium yellow squash, chopped
1-2	pounds sausage, mild or hot		
2	whole tomatoes, crushed	1	cup cabbage, chopped
2	(10 ounce) cans chicken broth	1	(15 ounce) can peas, drained
2	cups rice, uncooked		

In a large casserole pot, heat olive oil and sauté onion and bell pepper. When tender, add celery, garlic, oregano and bay leaves. Reduce heat and stew for 10 minutes. Add chopped sausage and cook for an additional 10 minutes. Stir in tomatoes, broth, rice, Worcestershire sauce and saffron. Salt and pepper to taste. Bring to a full boil for 10 minutes; remove from heat. Cover and bake at 350 degrees for 20 minutes. Stir in remaining vegetables. Bake for an additional 30 minutes or until all liquid is absorbed and vegetables are slightly crisp.

Yellow food coloring may be substituted for saffron.

Yield: 8 to 10 servings

In an average year, the Callaway Gardens Pastry Shop uses 104,260 pounds of flour, 36,508 pounds of sugar and 1,018,804 eggs!

Sister's Meat Balls

1	pound ground beef	½	teaspoon celery seed
6-8	saltine crackers, crushed		Flour
1	egg		Vegetable oil
1	onion, minced	1	can cream of mushroom soup
	Salt and pepper to taste		
⅛	teaspoon paprika	½	can water
⅛	teaspoon cayenne pepper	1	bay leaf

Mix together first 8 ingredients. Form into large balls, about the size of golf ball. Roll in flour and brown in vegetable oil on all sides. Mix soup and water; pour over meat balls. Add bay leaf and simmer 45 minutes to an hour. Remove and discard bay leaf. Serve meat balls over rice.

Yield: 10 to 12 meat balls depending upon size

❈ Ham and Veal Scaloppine

6	tablespoons butter	½	teaspoon savory
2	cups onions, chopped	3	cups cooked ham, julienne
3	pounds veal, cubed		sliced
	Flour	1	pound mushrooms, sliced
2	teaspoons salt	¼	cup butter
1	teaspoon garlic powder	4	cups sour cream
½	teaspoon marjoram		Noodles or spaghetti

In a large skillet, sauté onions in butter until golden brown. With a slotted spoon, remove onions from skillet and reserve. In the same butter, sauté the veal which has been cut into 1 inch squares dusted with flour. As the meat browns, more butter may need to be added. Sprinkle veal with salt, garlic powder, marjoram and savory. Add ham. Meanwhile, in a separate saucepan, sauté sliced mushrooms in ¼ cup butter and add to meat mixture. Heat until piping hot; add sour cream. Heat quickly without boiling, stirring all the while until smoothly blended. Do not allow the sour cream to curdle. Taste for seasoning and serve over hot buttered noodles or spaghetti.

Yield: 10 to 12 servings

More than 80 cubic yards of pine bark and 40 cubic yards of mushroom compost is used annually for fertilizing the Victory Garden and Butterfly Garden within Mr. Cason's Vegetable Garden.

Ham-Noodle Casserole

3½	tablespoons butter or	1	cup sour cream
	margarine	1	tablespoon tomato paste
1	cup chopped onion		Cooked ham
1	cup chopped green bell	8	ounces thin noodles, cooked
	pepper		Parmesan cheese
1	cup chopped celery		Paprika
2	(10¾ ounce) cans cream of		
	chicken soup, undiluted		

Sauté onion, pepper and celery in butter or margarine. In a double boiler, heat soup, sour cream and tomato paste, and pour over sautéed vegetables; add chunks of cooked ham. Mix well and add cooked noodles. Pour all ingredients into greased 9x13 inch casserole; sprinkle with Parmesan cheese and paprika. Bake at 350 degrees until bubbly.

You may wish to substitute dried chipped beef or crabmeat for the ham.

Yield: 15 servings

Ken's Chicken/Turkey Penne Pasta

2	tablespoons minced onion flakes	⅔	cup red wine
1	teaspoon instant minced garlic	2	tablespoons olive oil
2	teaspoons instant/low salt chicken bouillon	1	pound cooked, boneless chicken or turkey breast, cubed or in strips
2	teaspoons dried basil	1	cup mushrooms, sliced and cooked
1	(32 ounce) jar sun-dried tomato sauce	1	(16 ounce) package penne pasta
2	cups cooked chopped broccoli		Parmesan cheese (optional)

Combine onion, garlic, bouillon and basil in 2 to 3 ounces hot water. Mix and let stand 5 minutes. Combine sun-dried tomato sauce, broccoli, red wine, olive oil, chicken or turkey and mushrooms in a sauce pan. Add the mixture of onion, garlic, bouillon and basil. Heat for 10 minutes. (Do not boil). Cook penne pasta according to package instructions. Drain. Combine and mix penne pasta with the chicken/turkey mixture. Sprinkle with Parmesan cheese.

Recipe may be halved. Refrigerates and freezes well.

Yield: 4 to 6 servings

In 1995, parts of Callaway Gardens were ravaged when Hurricane Opal blew through the area with mighty winds. Remarkably, although 600 trees were blown down on the golf courses, none fell on the greens or tee boxes!

Spaghetti Pie

6	ounces vermicelli, cooked
½	clove garlic
¼	cup butter, melted
½	cup Parmesan cheese, freshly grated
1	large egg, beaten
1	tablespoon fresh basil, chopped
½	pound ground beef or turkey
¾	pound Italian sausage
½	cup chopped onion
1	(15 ounce) can tomato sauce
1	(6 ounce) can tomato paste
1	teaspoon sugar
2	tablespoons fresh basil, chopped
2	tablespoons fresh oregano, chopped
¼	cup white wine
1	cup ricotta cheese
6	ounces mozzarella cheese

To make the crust, combine vermicelli, garlic, butter, Parmesan cheese, egg and basil. Chop this mixture with a knife and press into a 10 inch pie plate. Prepare filling by cooking meats and onion together. Drain. Add tomato sauce, tomato paste, sugar, basil oregano and wine. Mix well. To assemble, spread ricotta on crust. Top with filling and cover with mozzarella cheese. Bake for 30 minutes at 350 degrees.

Yield: 8 servings

Lasagna

Cheese Layer

1	large egg	1	(18 ounce) carton low-fat cottage cheese

Sauce

1	medium onion, chopped	¼	teaspoon hot pepper sauce
1	medium bell pepper, chopped	1	(10¾ ounce) can tomato soup
1	medium garlic bulb, finely minced	¼	teaspoon chili powder
1	tablespoon cooking oil	1	tablespoon Worcestershire sauce
1½	pounds ground round steak	1	medium bay leaf
¾	teaspoon salt	8	ounces mozzarella cheese
½	teaspoon pepper	¼	cup grated Parmesan cheese
1	dash cayenne pepper	½	pound box lasagna noodles
1	dash basil		

Cheese layer: beat egg and stir in cottage cheese. Sauce: Cook onion, bell pepper and garlic in oil until tender. Add meat and stir until no longer pink. Mix in next 8 ingredients. Place bay leaf in middle of mixture. Place in 275 degree oven. Cover and cook 30 minutes, then remove bay leaf. Stir, cover and cook at least an hour. When sauce is ready, boil three quarts of water with salt and cooking oil. Add noodles and cook until tender. Drain. Spray two 8x8 inch glass casserole dishes with vegetable cooking spray. Spoon sauce barely covering bottom of dishes. Over sauce place layer of noodles, then a layer of mozzarella and sprinkle with Parmesan. Pour cottage cheese and egg mixture over it. Repeat sauce, noodles, mozzarella and thin layer of sauce with Parmesan sprinkled on top. Bake in 325 degree oven until bubbly (30 to 40 minutes). Remove from oven and let set for ½ hour.

This is a 35 year old family favorite.

Yield: 8 servings

"The dream of Callaway Gardens was my father's daily passion for the final ten years of his life. He dreamed of a clean, wholesome place where people of modest means would have a chance to see beauty. He dreamed of preserving the wild flowers of the Appalachian Mountains. He dreamed of setting an example in the South and throughout the nation for environmental and conservation methods of managing the earth for the benefit of future generations. He dreamed of private initiatives to show the way for public institutions to be more productive."
— *Bo Callaway*

Spinach-Stuffed Manicotti

1   (8 ounce) box manicotti shells, uncooked
    Vegetable cooking spray
¾   cup diced onion
¾   cup diced green pepper
2   (14¼ ounce) cans no-salt added whole tomatoes, undrained and chopped
1   (8 ounce) can no-salt added tomato sauce
1   (6 ounce) can no-salt added tomato paste
1   tablespoon brown sugar
1   teaspoon dried whole oregano
½   teaspoon salt

¼   teaspoon pepper
2   (10 ounce) packages frozen chopped spinach, thawed and drained
1   (15 ounce) carton part-skim ricotta cheese
1   (4 ounce) package part-skim shredded mozzarella cheese
3   tablespoons Parmesan cheese, grated
2   teaspoons dried Italian seasoning
¼   teaspoon nutmeg
¼   teaspoon pepper

Cook manicotti shells according to package directions, omitting salt and fat. Drain well and set aside. Coat a large sauce pan with cooking spray. Place over medium-high heat until hot. Add onion and green pepper; sauté until tender. Stir in tomato and next 6 ingredients. Bring to a boil; cover, reduce heat and simmer 20 minutes, stirring occasionally. Drain spinach; press between paper towels until barely moist. Combine spinach, ricotta cheese and remaining ingredients in a medium bowl; stir well. Spoon spinach/cheese mixture evenly into manicotti shells. Spoon half tomato mixture into 9x13 inch dish coated with cooking spray. Place shells in dish; top with remaining tomato mixture. Cover and bake at 350 degrees for 40 to 45 minutes or until thoroughly heated.

Yield: 12 servings

Charlie's Chili

2	pounds ground beef	5	whole cloves
2	medium onions, chopped	1	ounce chili powder
2	(14½ ounce) cans tomatoes	½	teaspoon cayenne pepper
1	(11.5 ounce) can tomato		(or to taste)
	juice	2	(15½ ounce) cans kidney
2	bay leaves		beans

Brown ground beef and chopped onions together in skillet. Boil tomatoes and tomato juice in 6 quart boiler for 15 to 20 minutes. Add bay leaves, cloves, chili powder, cayenne pepper, kidney beans and ground beef/onion mixture. Simmer for 30 minutes. Remove and discard bay leaves before serving.

Yield: 8 to 10 servings

Sometimes called red pepper, cayenne is available as ground or crushed. It is used in spice blends, barbecue ribs and chili. It should be used cautiously, as a very small amount can add a fiery element to any dish.

Delicious Spaghetti Sauce

6	tablespoons olive oil	2	tablespoons oregano
⅓-½	cup butter or margarine	2	teaspoons basil
1	medium onion, chopped	2	bay leaves
3	cloves garlic, minced	3	teaspoons sugar
1	cup grated carrot		Freshly ground black
1	cup chopped celery		pepper
3	cups sliced fresh mushrooms	4	teaspoons parsley
½	cup chopped green pepper	1	teaspoon salt
2	(28 ounce) cans Italian	1	cup dry red wine
	plum tomatoes	1	pound ground beef
2	(28 ounce) cans stewed	2	pounds sweet Italian bulk
	tomatoes		sausage
1	(12 ounce) can tomato paste		

In a large pot (8 to 10 quart) heat olive oil and butter. Sauté onions and garlic in oil; add carrots, green pepper, celery and mushrooms. Cut up or mash tomatoes; add with juice. Add tomato paste, spices and wine. In skillet, brown ground beef and sausage; drain and add to sauce mixture. Cook uncovered for 2 to 3 hours over low heat, stirring occasionally.

Yield: 5 to 6 quarts (20 servings)

Chile Rellenos

2	(4 ounce) cans green chiles, drained and chopped	10	eggs, beaten
¾	cup self-rising flour	3	cups large curd cottage cheese
1	teaspoon baking powder	3	cups grated Monterey jack cheese

Mix all ingredients together thoroughly. Place in casserole dish and cook for 25 minutes at 325 degrees or until set.

Serve with cornbread and Avocado Grapefruit Salad.

Yield: 10 to 12 servings, depending on appetites

Mexican Casserole

1	pound ground beef	1	(10-12) package tortillas
1	(8 ounce) jar mild salsa	1	cup shredded cheddar cheese
½	cup sour cream		
1	(2 ounce) jar pimientos		

Brown and drain ground beef. Mix ground beef, salsa, sour cream and pimientos. Cut tortillas into strips and cover 8x8 inch square casserole dish with half of the strips. Add half of ground beef mixture. Repeat layers and top with 1 cup shredded cheese. Bake at 350 degrees about 30 minutes.

Yield: 6 servings

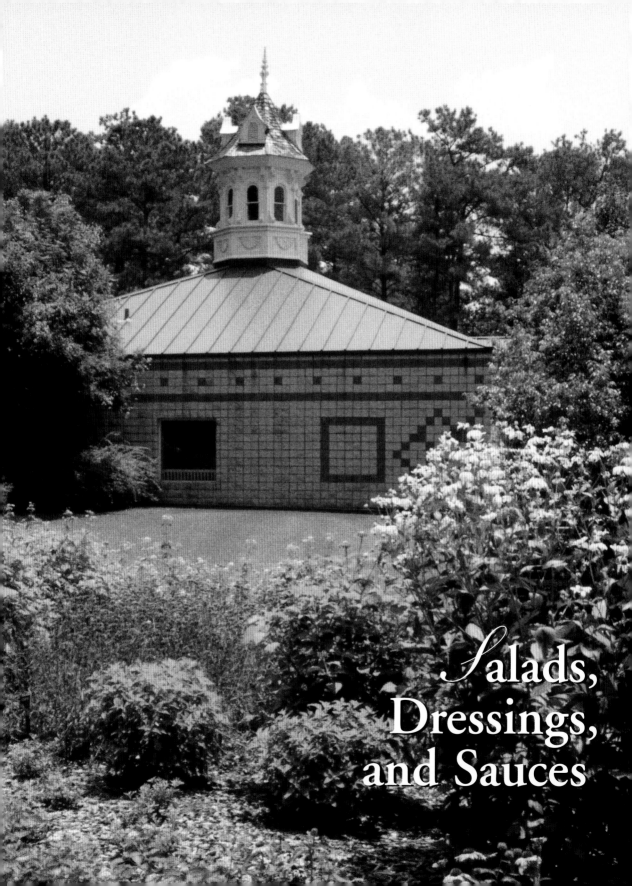

Salads,
Dressings,
and Sauces

Cecil B. Day Butterfly Center

Flights of fancy . . .

. . . the term *flights of fancy* takes on new meaning in Callaway Gardens' Cecil B. Day Butterfly Center where 1,000 tropical butterflies fly freely through the air. Guests stroll along a winding path as the butterflies flutter delightfully around them.

Tropical plants and birds, including enchanting hummingbirds, reside peacefully with the colorful winged jewels in this grand, glass-enclosed tropical conservatory.

Before you ever reach the conservatory, a walk through the Center's lobby introduces you to the world of one of nature's most delicate and intriguing creatures. A hand-tufted rug on the lobby floor depicts Georgia's state butterfly, the Eastern Tiger Swallowtail. The rug's border is adorned by images of tropical butterflies, similar to those seen in the conservatory. Overhead an intricate copper chandelier hangs gracefully over the lobby. The chandelier depicts a native passionflower, a host plant for many butterflies. Nearby, a gift shop features a bounty of gifts, jewelry, toys and home decor items all themed around butterflies, birds and insects.

Every day visitors are awed and inspired by the Cecil B. Day Butterfly Center and the rare beauty that it holds inside.

Avocado-Grapefruit Salad

Salad

4	large grapefruit (or one large jar of sections)	2	heads Bibb lettuce
2	large avocados	1	package blue cheese, crumbled (optional)

Celery Seed Dressing

1	teaspoon dry mustard	⅛	teaspoon red pepper
1	teaspoon grated onion	⅓	cup sugar
1	teaspoon celery seed	4	tablespoons vinegar
	Salt and fresh ground pepper to taste	1	cup oil

Cool six salad plates in refrigerator. Peel and section grapefruit, or drain jar of grapefruit sections. Peel and slice avocado. Arrange lettuce on cooled plates. Arrange grapefruit and avocado on lettuce. Just before serving, add celery seed dressing, and sprinkle with blue cheese. To prepare dressing: combine all dry ingredients. Alternately add, oil and vinegar, stirring briskly. Refrigerate.

This is light, cool and refreshing.

Yield: 6 servings

Although most people drive through Callaway Gardens, one of the best ways to enjoy it is by biking along the 10-mile Discovery Bicycle Trail. This winding trail with gentle hills takes bicyclists by all the major attractions and gives riders an up-close encounter with nature.

Artichoke Salad

2	cups cooked brown rice	½	cup mayonnaise
	Chicken broth	2	(8 ounce) jars marinated artichoke hearts
1	tablespoon chopped onion		
½	chopped green pepper	¼	teaspoon curry powder
8	chopped pimiento olives		

Cook rice in chicken broth. Cool; add onion, pepper and olives. Mix mayonnaise with liquid from drained artichokes and curry powder until blended. Add to rice with finely chopped artichoke hearts. Mix, refrigerate until well chilled.

Yield: 8 servings

Black-Eyed Pea Salad

2	(15 ounce) cans black-eyed peas, drained	¼	cup chopped parsley
1	(15 ounce) can white hominy (optional)	¼	cup cider vinegar
1	Vidalia® onion, chopped	½	cup canola oil
2	large tomatoes	1	jalapeño pepper, finely chopped
			Salt to taste

Combine peas, hominy, onion, tomato and parsley in a large bowl. In medium bowl, whisk vinegar, oil, jalapeño and salt. Pour over vegetables and toss evenly to distribute dressing. Serve on lettuce leaves with parsley sprigs and thin slices of jalapeño peppers.

Yield: 8 servings

At Mr. Cason's Vegetable Garden, 20 to 30 varieties of looseleaf, butterhead and romaine lettuce are grown.

Sweet and Crunchy Broccoli Salad

1	pound bacon	½	cup sunflower seeds
1	large head broccoli	1	cup mayonnaise
½	head cauliflower (optional)	½	cup sugar
1	medium red onion	2	tablespoons vinegar
1	cup raisins		

Fry bacon until crispy and crumble. Chop broccoli and cauliflower into small chunks. Slice onion and chop into fine pieces. Add to vegetables. Add raisins, sunflower seeds and bacon. Mix mayonnaise, sugar, and vinegar. Mix well with salad. Chill.

Yield: 12 servings

Tumi Salad

1	head red cabbage, shredded	¼	cup sunflower seeds
1	head green cabbage, shredded	¼	cup sugar
6	green onions, sliced	½	teaspoon pepper
2	(3 ounce) packages Ramen noodles, crushed	1	tablespoon sesame oil
¾	cup slivered almonds	6	tablespoons rice vinegar
		4	tablespoons oil
		2	packages Ramen seasoning

Mix together cabbages, onions, and crushed noodles. Set aside. Roast almonds and sunflower seeds on a cookie sheet, at 325 degrees for 10 minutes. Shake together remaining ingredients. Combine all ingredients.

Yield: 12 servings

" I don't know what the soul is, but whatever it is, a sense of beauty and goodness must be at the heart of it."
— Cason J. Callaway

Giardiniera Marinated Vegetable Salad

1½	cups wine vinegar	1	cup each; parboiled carrots, cauliflower, zucchini, yellow squash, green, yellow and red bell peppers, mushrooms and celery
1	cup salad or olive oil		
6	tablespoons sugar		
2	teaspoons salt		
2	teaspoons black pepper		
1	teaspoon oregano		Black and green olives, as desired
½	cup water		

Bring first 7 ingredients to a boil. Add all cut vegetables except olives. Bring to a second boil and boil exactly 5 minutes. Remove from heat, stir in olives, cover and let cool. Refrigerate. Will keep 2-3 weeks.

Other vegetables of your choice may be added.

This is great for picnics, tailgating parties, backyard barbecues or any other fun function! Everyone likes this one!

Yield: 18 servings

Sugar Snap Pea and Cantaloupe Salad

Salad

¾	pound sugar snap peas	½	bunch watercress
1	small cantaloupe		Toasted slivered almonds for garnish

Cream Sherry Vinaigrette (Makes 2 cups)

¼	cup egg substitute	1	clove garlic, crushed
2	tablespoons fresh lemon juice	½	teaspoon dried tarragon
2	tablespoons red wine vinegar	½	teaspoon anchovy paste
1	tablespoon sherry	¼	teaspoon salt
		¼	teaspoon pepper
		1½	cups vegetable oil

Remove strings from peas, cut in half diagonally and blanch 1 minute. Rinse with cold water. Peel and seed cantaloupe; then cut into slices (½ to 2 inches thick). Remove stems from watercress, tear into 2 inch pieces. Mix peas, cantaloupe, watercress and toasted almonds. Combine all ingredients for vinaigrette, except oil, in food processor. Add oil slowly while blade is on. Serve vinaigrette on the side.

This is a great summer lunch or supper salad!

Yield: 8 servings

Chicken Salad with Rice and Fruit

2½	cups cooked chicken, cubed	½	cup mandarin oranges, drained
1½	cups cooked white rice	½	cup slivered almonds or pecans, toasted
¾	cup small green grapes	1	cup ranch salad dressing
¾	cup celery, sliced	½	teaspoon salt
½	cup pineapple tidbits, drained		

Combine all ingredients in a large bowl. Toss gently. May be made the night before. Store in an airtight container in the refrigerator. Serve on lettuce with crackers.

Yield: 12 servings

Strawberry and Spinach Salad

Salad

1	pound tender young (or baby) spinach	1	pint strawberries, washed, hulled and sliced
		⅓	cup Poppy Seed Dressing

Poppy Seed Dressing (Makes 1 cup)

¼	cup granulated sugar	¼	teaspoon salt
¼	cup rice vinegar	½	cup vegetable oil
1	teaspoon grated onion	1½	tablespoons poppy seeds
½	teaspoon dry mustard		

Shred the spinach. Place spinach and berries in a large bowl. To prepare dressing, combine sugar and vinegar in a small saucepan and stir over low heat 2 or 3 minutes until sugar is dissolved. Remove from heat and add onion, mustard and salt. Whisk in oil until well blended. Stir in poppy seeds. Pour dressing in a jar, cover lightly and refrigerate. Add about ⅓ cup dressing to salad and toss well before serving.

Yield: 6 servings

"All I have done is try to fix it so that anybody who came here would see something beautiful wherever he might look."
— Cason J. Callaway

 # *German Potato Salad*

Salad

2	pounds potatoes	4-6	strips bacon, cooked and crumbled
½	cup chicken or beef stock		
½	onion, chopped		

Dressing

6	tablespoons wine vinegar	½	teaspoon freshly ground pepper
6	tablespoons vegetable oil		
1	teaspoons salt	1	egg yolk

Wash potatoes and boil until tender. Cool, peel and slice. Pour stock over potatoes. Allow time for stock to be absorbed, then add onion. Mix remaining ingredients except bacon, beat well. Pour over potatoes. Sprinkle crumbled bacon on top. Serve hot or cold. Delicious!

Yield: 4 servings

Roasted New Potato Salad with Rosemary

Salad

2   pounds baby new potatoes
¼   cup olive oil
3   tablespoons chopped fresh rosemary

Salt and cracked pepper to taste
Fresh rosemary for garnish

Dressing

2   tablespoons white wine
3   tablespoons mayonnaise
1   tablespoon white wine vinegar
1   teaspoon Dijon mustard

2   green onions, sliced thin
3   tablespoons chopped parsley
Salt and pepper to taste

Preheat oven to 450 degrees. Cook potatoes in boiling water (about 10 minutes) until just crisp. Drain. Cut potatoes into quarters. Place on baking sheet and toss with olive oil. Sprinkle chopped rosemary on potatoes. Mix. Sprinkle with salt and pepper. Put into hot oven and roast until they are browned and crisp. Check every 5 minutes. It should take about 20 minutes. Mix all dressing ingredients and toss with potatoes. Garnish with fresh rosemary to serve. The secret is the dressing!

Use this roasting method with almost any vegetable, or grill instead of oven roasting.

Yield: 10 servings

Cucumber Mousse

2   (3 ounce) packages lemon flavored gelatin
1   cup boiling water
2   cucumbers, unpeeled
1   small onion

¾   cup mayonnaise
1½ cups cottage cheese
½   cup sour cream
2   teaspoons vinegar
1   cup chopped pecans (optional)

Dissolve gelatin in boiling water and cool. Grate cucumbers and onion and drain well. Add to gelatin. In food processor, mix remaining ingredients except chopped pecans. Fold into gelatin and mix in nuts. Put in mold to congeal.

Yield: 12 servings

Minted Wild Rice Salad

Salad

1	cup wild rice, uncooked	⅔	cup raisins
1	green bell pepper, chopped	⅔	cup coarsely chopped pecans
8	green onions, chopped		
½	cup chopped fresh mint	2	tomatoes, chopped

Dressing

½	cup fresh lemon juice	½	teaspoon ground pepper
½	cup olive oil	¼	teaspoon salt

Cook rice according to directions on box. Drain and cool. Add remaining ingredients. Mix dressing ingredients and combine with rice mixture. Marinate several hours.

Good for a summer buffet dinner!

Yield: 8 to 10 servings

"In his mind's eye, Cason saw here a beautiful garden, and he made it, and it will always be his, a reflection of his personality."
— Bo Callaway

Mrs. Batson's Old Fashioned Pressed Chicken

5	cups cooked chicken, ground	2	teaspoons grated lemon rind
		1	teaspoon lemon juice
2	hard-boiled eggs, grated	2	tablespoons grated onions
2	cups chicken broth, cook as directed below	2	teaspoons celery salt
		1	teaspoon white pepper
1	cup real mayonnaise	1	teaspoon paprika

Grind (or grate) chicken and eggs very fine. Cook down chicken broth the day before. Chill and be sure it congeals. Warm and mix with other ingredients. Salt to taste. Place in oiled container and chill. When it becomes firm, put a weighted object (foiled wrapped brick) to press down. It will be very soft until it congeals. Slice to serve.

Use bread pan to make a loaf.

Yield: 8 servings

Curried Chicken Salad on Pastry Shell

Salad

1⅔ cups mayonnaise	3 whole chicken breasts, cooked and diced
¼ cup heavy cream	1 can water chestnuts, drained and sliced
2 tablespoons lemon juice	⅓ pound pea pods, blanched for 1 minute and chilled
1 teaspoon curry powder, or to taste	Tomato wedges and chopped Italian parsley for garnish
Salt to taste	
¾ cup cooked rice	
1 cup diced celery	
2 tablespoons chopped parsley	

Pastry Shell

⅔ cup water	⅔ cup flour
5 tablespoons butter	3 eggs
¼ teaspoon salt	

Combine mayonnaise, cream, lemon juice, curry powder and salt for dressing. Combine rice, celery and parsley. Toss with chicken. Add dressing and chestnuts. For Pastry Shell, combine water, butter and salt. Bring to a boil. Add flour all at once and remove from heat. Beat with wire whisk. Put into food processor, add eggs and process until smooth. Pour into ungreased 10 inch springform pan, spread over bottom and ¾ up on sides. Bake at 400 degrees until puffed and brown. Prick shell in 10 places and return to cooling oven for 10 minutes. Remove from pan. To assemble: Line side and bottom of shell with pea pods; add chicken salad. Garnish with tomato wedges and chopped parsley.

Yield: 10 servings

Marinated Herbed Tomato Salad

Salad

6	tomatoes cut into wedges	1	large onion, sliced
3	bell peppers, sliced or chunked	1	cup pitted ripe olives

Dressing

⅔	cup vegetable oil	1	teaspoon sugar
¼	cup vinegar	1	teaspoon salt
¼	cup fresh parsley, snipped	½	teaspoon dried basil
¼	cup green onions with tops, snipped	½	teaspoon dried marjoram
		¼	teaspoon pepper

Combine vegetables and olives. Combine dressing ingredients in a jar with tight fitting lid. Shake well. Pour over vegetables. Cover and refrigerate 3 to 4 hours.

Yield: 6 servings

Asparagus Congealed Salad

2	envelopes unflavored gelatin	½	teaspoon salt
½	cup cold water	¾	cup finely chopped celery
¾	cup sugar	½	cup chopped pecans
½	cup white vinegar	1	(10.5 ounce) can asparagus tips, cut
1¼	cups liquid (asparagus liquid and water)	2	tablespoons lemon juice
2	envelopes unflavored gelatin	1	(4 ounce) jar pimientos, chopped
½	cup cold water		

Soften gelatin in cold water. Mix sugar, vinegar and liquid. Bring to a boil and add gelatin, stirring to dissolve. Place in refrigerator until it begins to congeal. Add other ingredients. Return to refrigerator to complete congealing.

Reduce celery to ½ cup. Add ½ cup each tiny green peas, French cut green beans, asparagus tips, sliced stuffed green olives and one very small chopped onion along with the lemon juice and a 2 ounce jar pimientos. Leave out the pecans. Serve on lettuce leaves on individual plates with a dollop of dressing made by mixing ½ cup mayonnaise, 1 tablespoon horseradish and ½ cup sour cream.

Yield: 8 servings

It takes a body to tell time in the Herb Garden in Mr. Cason's Vegetable Garden. Using the analemmatic dial, a person stands in a specific spot and raises an arm. Their arm casts a shadow across the appropriate hour plate on the ground, indicating the time. Of course, during daylight savings time, the time must be adjusted by an hour.

Egg Tuna Mold

1	cup mayonnaise	6	eggs, hard-boiled and
½	cup sour cream		chopped
½	cup milk	1	(7 ounce) can white meat
1	tablespoon lemon juice		tuna
½	teaspoon curry powder	1	cup chopped celery
1	envelope plus 1½ teaspoon	3	tablespoons chopped onion
	unflavored gelatin	1	cup stuffed olives, chopped
¾	cup water	1	dash hot sauce
1	chicken bouillon cube		Black pepper to taste

Combine mayonnaise, sour cream, milk, lemon juice and curry powder in a bowl. Soften gelatin in water; add bouillon cube and stir over low heat until gelatin and cube are dissolved. Cool slightly, stir in all ingredients. Chill until slightly thickened, put in oiled ring mold and chill until set.

Yield: 8 servings

Salmon Mousse

2	envelopes unflavored gelatin	1	cup finely chopped cucumber
1½	cups cold water	1	tablespoon finely chopped
1	cup mayonnaise		onion
1	cup sour cream	½	teaspoon dill weed
1	scant tablespoon lemon juice		Salt and pepper to taste
1	(14¾ ounce) can red		
	salmon, cleaned		

Soften gelatin in water. Stir over low heat to dissolve. Cool. Thoroughly combine mayonnaise and sour cream. Add lemon juice. Stir in gelatin. Chill until slightly thickened. Fold in salmon, cucumber, onion, dill, salt and pepper. Pour into a 5 cup mold (fish mold, if available). Chill to set. Unmold on a bed of lettuce or spinach. Garnish with sliced olive for eyes and thin slices of lemon.

Lemon yogurt may be substituted for sour cream and lemon juice.

Yield: 12 servings

1000 Islands Dressing

1	cup mayonnaise	1	teaspoon pimiento, chopped
1	teaspoon chopped green pepper	1	large hard-boiled egg, chopped
3	tablespoons chili sauce	1	teaspoon chopped chives
1	teaspoon green olives, chopped		Salt and pepper to taste

Mix, chill and serve with your favorite salad.

This is the original 1000 Islands Dressing which gets its name from the '1,000' islands of upstate New York!

Yield: 4 to 6 servings

"Callaway Gardens is a special place where families can enjoy the companionship of nature."
— *Lady Bird Johnson*

Fruit Salad Dressing

½	cup sugar	1	teaspoon finely grated onion
1	teaspoon salt	1	cup olive oil
1	teaspoon dry mustard	⅓	cup white vinegar
1	teaspoon celery seed		
1	teaspoon paprika		

Mix dry ingredients and add onion. Add oil and vinegar a little at a time. Beat to blend. Keep in refrigerator. Wonderful over grapefruit and avocado sections.

Yield: 1¾ cups

Honey-Mustard Dressing

⅓	cup honey	2	tablespoons fresh lemon juice
¼	cup Dijon mustard	¼	cup rice vinegar
1	clove garlic, peeled and minced	1	cup canola oil
		½	teaspoon sesame oil

In a blender or food processor, combine honey, mustard, garlic, lemon juice and vinegar. Process until well mixed, about 1 minute. With the motor running, add the oils in a slow, steady stream, processing until the dressing is smooth, with a creamy texture. Store, covered in refrigerator. The flavor will improve if made several hours before using.

If the dressing becomes too thick, whisk in a couple of tablespoons of water.

Yield: Approximately 1½ cups

Johnny Burke's Roquefort Dressing

½	pound Roquefort cheese		Salt and pepper to taste
1	pint real mayonnaise	1	button garlic, chopped very fine
1	ounce vinegar		

Grind (or mash) Roquefort to paste. Add mayonnaise and whip. Add vinegar and whip thoroughly. Add salt, pepper and garlic. If necessary, thin down with coffee cream.

A good grade of bleu cheese may be substituted for the Roquefort.

Johnny Burke was chef at the Last Frontier Hotel in Las Vegas, Nevada in 1954.

Yield: 2½ to 3 cups

Blender Pesto Sauce for the Freezer

2	cups basil leaves		2	cloves garlic, peeled
⅓	cup olive oil		⅔	cup Parmesan cheese,
2	tablespoons pine nuts			freshly grated

This may be made ahead and frozen for convenience. Blend the first four ingredients until smooth. Freeze in ice cube trays. Cover with plastic wrap. When solid, store cubes in ziplock bags. When ready to use, thaw to room temperature. Beat in cheese, using 1 tablespoon per cube to avoid separating. Use 4 cubes for each ½ pound pasta. Cook pasta. When it is done, add 1 teaspoon hot water to the pesto and stir until smooth. Serve warm, not hot, or it will curdle.

This is also good on baked Irish potatoes.

Yield: 12 one tablespoon size cubes. Enough for 1½ pounds of pasta.

" ...surely the purpose to uplift and regenerate the spirit of man by the beauty of the environment is the work of the Lord."
— *John A. Sibley*

Barbecue Sauce

¼	cup diced onion			Juice of 2 lemons
2	cups apple cider vinegar		¼	cup butter or margarine
4	cups ketchup		2	teaspoons cayenne pepper
1½	cups prepared mustard			(may be adjusted to taste)
½	cup plus 2 tablespoons		2	teaspoons black pepper
	Worcestershire sauce			

Put onion and vinegar in a blender or food processor and blend to liquefy. Mix this with remaining ingredients in a 3 quart saucepan and simmer for one hour.

Use for poultry, beef or pork.

Yield: 2½ quarts

BBQue Sauce

1	(44 ounce) bottle ketchup	6	large drops hot sauce
1½	ounces Worcestershire sauce	5	tablespoons mustard
2	ounces liquid barbecue smoke	1	teaspoon black pepper
		1	teaspoon lemon or lime juice

Mix all together thoroughly. Keep in refrigerator in a glass bottle or jar until ready to use. Age just makes mixture better.

Yield: 1½ quarts

> *"I'm convinced the Prunifolia azalea would be extinct today without the preservation efforts of Cason and Virginia Callaway."*
> — *Tavia C. McCuen (The Nature Conservancy of Georgia)*

Ruth Stevens' Barbecue Sauce

1	pound margarine	2	cups tomato catsup
½	gallon chicken broth	½	bottle Worcestershire sauce
2	cups sugar	3	lemons, sliced
1	tablespoon pepper	1	teaspoon clove
1	teaspoon allspice	1	teaspoon ginger
1	teaspoon cinnamon		Salt and pepper, to taste

Melt margarine. Add all ingredients. Boil until it thickens.

Ruth Stevens of Warm Springs prepared this sauce for the Barbecue which had been planned for President Franklin Delano Roosevelt, Thursday, April 12, 1945, the day he died.

Yield: About 2½ quarts

Tomato Chili Sauce

7	cups peeled and diced fresh ripe tomatoes	½	teaspoon ground cayenne pepper
2	cups diced onions	1½	cups sugar
3½	teaspoons salt	1	cup diced bell pepper
½	teaspoon black pepper	⅓	cup vinegar
¼	cup hot green peppers, diced very small		

Mix all ingredients in a 12 to 14 quart boiler. Boil slowly until thick. When cool, place in covered container and refrigerate. Will keep for several days in the refrigerator. Delicious on vegetables and/or meats!

It is advisable to wear gloves when cutting hot peppers, and hold by the stems. DO NOT TOUCH FACE OR EYES BEFORE WASHING HANDS THOROUGHLY!!!

Washing hands in milk will take heat out of hot peppers left on skin.

Yield: Approximately 4 pints

"All who come will be heirs to the richness of this natural area."
— Virginia H. Callaway

Plum Sauce

2	quarts ripe plums	½	teaspoon ground cinnamon
2	pounds sugar	½	teaspoon ground cloves
1	cup vinegar	½	teaspoon ground allspice

Wash, pit and chop plums. Combine sugar and vinegar. Bring to a boil, reduce heat and add plums. Cook until thick and syrupy, about 1½ hours, being careful it does not stick to the bottom of the boiler. Remove from heat. Add spices and mix well.

Yield: 4 pints

Raisin Sauce

⅓ cup raisins
½ cup water
⅓ cup currant jelly
½ teaspoon grated orange
   peel

½ cup orange juice
2 tablespoons brown sugar
1 tablespoon cornstarch
1 dash allspice
1 dash salt

Combine first 5 ingredients in a saucepan. Bring just to the boiling point. Combine remaining ingredients and stir into raisin mixture. Cook and stir until thick and bubbly. Serve warm. Delicious with ham!

Yield: 2 cups

Soups,
Stews and
Sandwiches

Fantasy In Lights®

...the holiday tradition of the South!

Take millions of colored lights, festive
holiday music, animation, an open-air trolley
and a chilly winter's night and you've got the
makings for a spirited holiday celebration
called Fantasy In Lights. Fantasy In Lights at
Callaway Gardens started in 1992 with a
handful of larger-than-life scenes and an
outdoor Christmas Village. Today, it features
more than a dozen lighted and animated
scenes along a five-mile drive, a 22,000-
square foot indoor Christmas Village, the
Fantasy Café and the Trim-A-Tree Shop.

Though it takes just an evening to enjoy
Fantasy In Lights, the heightened spirits
linger through the holiday season. That's why
so many families always include Fantasy In
Lights as part of their Christmas tradition.

Blender Gazpacho

1   (10 ounce) can, plus 2½ cups, vegetable juice cocktail, divided
1   cucumber, peeled, seeded, chopped and divided
2   tomatoes, peeled, chopped and divided

1   tablespoon sugar
½   cup white wine vinegar
½   cup olive oil
1   onion, finely chopped
    Croutons, chopped green pepper, diced hard-boiled egg white for garnish

Combine 10 ounce can juice, ½ cucumber, 1 tomato, sugar, vinegar and olive oil in blender and blend. Add 2½ cups juice, the second tomato, ½ cucumber and onion. Garnish with croutons, green pepper and egg white.

Yield: 8 servings

Cold Cucumber Soup

3   cucumbers, divided
2   tablespoons butter
1   leek, sliced
1   bay leaf
1   tablespoon flour
3   cups chicken broth

    Salt and pepper to taste
1   cup cream
    Juice of ½ lemon
1   teaspoon fresh dill or mint, finely chopped

Peel 2 cucumbers and sauté gently in 2 tablespoons butter with 1 leek (white part only) and 1 bay leaf for 20 minutes or until tender. Stir in flour. Add 3 cups chicken broth, salt and pepper, simmer for 30 minutes. Blend and strain. Chill. Add 1 cucumber peeled, seeded and grated, cream and the juice of 1 lemon. Stir in finely chopped dill or mint.

Yield: 6 servings

It takes a lot of manpower to put Fantasy In Lights® together. Each scene takes approximately six weeks to build, and it takes six weeks to install the entire show. Callaway Gardens "elves" can be seen as early as late September installing the various scenes around the five-mile Scenic Drive.

Cold Peach Soup

4	large ripe peaches	¼	teaspoon curry powder
2	cups dry white wine	3	cloves
1	cup water		Sour cream
3	tablespoons sugar		Orange slices
¼	teaspoon cinnamon		Fresh mint

*Fantasy In Lights
uses more than
three million light bulbs,
40 miles of power cable
and 65,000 feet
of sound cable.*

Peel and halve peaches. Purée in blender or food processor. Put purée in saucepan; add wine, water, sugar and spices. Bring to boil and simmer 10 minutes, stirring. Remove cloves and chill at least 4 hours. Serve in chilled bowls with a thick slice of orange and a dollop of sour cream with a sprig of mint.

To use as a dessert, add 1 pint of heavy cream immediately before serving in place of sour cream.

Yield: 4 servings

Cold Raspberry Soup

1½	tablespoons unflavored gelatin	1½	cups pineapple juice
⅓	cup cold water	1⅓	cups half-and-half
¾	cup hot water	1⅓	cups Harvey's Bristol Cream (do not substitute)
4	cups fresh or frozen raspberries, puréed	⅓	cup grenadine
3½	cups sour cream		Juice of one lemon
			Sugar to taste

Soak gelatin in cold water for 5 minutes. Stir in hot water and dissolve gelatin over low heat. Combine with remaining ingredients and place them in a stainless steel container. Cover and refrigerate overnight. Garnish with a few whole raspberries, if desired.

Yield: 24 servings

Chicken-Rice Soup

1	bag instant rice	2	large onions, chopped fine
4	(14.5 ounce) cans chicken broth	4	tablespoons margarine
2	ribs celery, finely sliced	⅛	teaspoon pepper
2	carrots, scraped and finely sliced	½	teaspoon salt

Cook rice. (3 cups regular cooked rice may be substituted) While rice is cooking, bring 1 can chicken broth to a boil; add celery, carrots, onions and margarine. Reduce heat and simmer, covered, for 10 minutes. In a large saucepan, combine all ingredients and bring to a boil. Reduce heat and simmer for only 5 minutes.

Variation: Add 2 boiled, chopped boneless chicken breasts.

Yield: 6 servings

Oak timbers used in the original Club House, Information Center and Overlook Pavilion were cut from Callaway Property as were the original wood shakes.

Lima Bean Chowder

1	pound hot sausage	1	clove garlic, peeled
1	large onion, diced	1½	cups frozen baby lima beans
3	cups chicken broth	¼	teaspoon freshly ground black pepper
1	cup thinly sliced carrots	1½	cups light cream
2	cups cubed potatoes		Dill weed sprigs
2	cups sliced fresh mush-rooms		

Cook sausage; drain well. Add onion and sauté. Add broth, carrots, potatoes, mushrooms, whole clove garlic, lima beans and pepper. Cover and cook for 25 minutes. Stir in cream and heat until hot. Remove garlic. Serve garnished with sprig of dill weed.

Yield: 12 servings

Fresh Broccoli Soup

1	large head broccoli cut into medium size chunks, using most of the stem	2	cups milk
1	medium potato, quartered	½	cup fresh squeezed orange juice
1	carrot, quartered	1	cup dry Marsala wine
1	medium onion, quartered	2	cups grated Jarlsberg or Danish Cream Havarti cheese
5	large cloves garlic		
2	ribs celery cut in 2 inch lengths		Sea salt to taste
1	quart chicken stock		Freshly ground pepper to taste

Callaway Gardens was originally conceived as a private facility of homesites, lakes, clubhouse and golf course. After seeing the Gardens begin to take shape, Cason Callaway told longtime friend Bill Cooksey, "This is a beautiful place. Virginia and I were talking last night and we feel it is going to be too beautiful for so few people to enjoy. So we're going to ... make it a place for the public to enjoy."

Put the first seven ingredients of vegetables and stock into a heavy bottomed soup pot and boil 6 minutes or until the vegetables are still very firm but cooked. Do not overcook, as vital nutrients will be lost. The vegetables should be cooked enough that they will not create a strain on your blender. Send all of the cooked vegetables through a blender with just enough broth to blend easily and thoroughly. Do not fill the blender too full. Blend about 1 minute per blender full. Return stock and puréed vegetables to soup pot on low heat. Add milk, orange juice and Marsala and heat thoroughly. Add the grated cheese, stirring constantly until melted. Season with sea salt and freshly ground pepper. You may wish to add more garlic or Marsala, or may desire a thicker consistency. To thicken, melt ¼ cup butter in a small saucepan, add ¼ cup flour and whisk over medium heat for 1½ minutes; add immediately to hot soup, whisking briskly to ensure no lumps develop. DO NOT LET THE SOUP BOIL AT ANY POINT. Serve with a choice of garnish: Grated Romano cheese, garlic croutons, bacon bits or chopped egg.

Vegetable stock may be substituted for the chicken stock. Dieters may use water. For a richer flavor, use half-and-half. Dieters, use skim milk.

For a "LIGHT WINTER PICNIC IN THE GARDENS" we suggest putting soup in a thermos and serve with German White Wine Mosel Blumchen, ham biscuits and apples, pears, grapes and Gourmandise cheese.

Yield: 8 servings

Low Country Bazaar Okra Soup

2   pounds beef (short ribs or chuck)
2   onions, finely chopped
2   (10 ounce) boxes frozen okra, thawed

2   (28 ounce) cans peeled tomatoes
1   slice bacon
      Salt and pepper to taste
1   bay leaf
½   cup white rice

Cover meat and onions with 3 to 4 quarts of water. Bring to a boil, reduce heat and cover. Simmer on low for 2 hours. Add okra, tomatoes, bacon, salt and pepper. Cook covered, another two hours on low heat. Stir and cook down until it reaches a stew consistency. Cook rice. Spoon soup over rice in individual bowls. Soup can be cooked all day, adding extra water as needed.

Rice may be cooked in with the soup 30 minutes before serving. 3½ pounds fresh, peeled tomatoes may be substituted for canned tomatoes. Three pounds fresh okra, washed, stemmed and chopped fine, may substitute for the frozen okra.

Corn muffins are good with this soup.

Yield: 10 to 12 cups

"Many Americans of our generation have lived by utopian dreams. I know of none more sincere than Cason Callaway in complete devotion to the hope that his life might actually bring Utopia one step closer to the grasp of men."
— Paul Schubert,
Cason Callaway of Blue Springs

Potato Soup

5   medium potatoes, peeled and cubed
5   cups water
¾   teaspoon salt, divided
1   small carrot, scraped and sliced thin
1   medium onion, finely chopped

1   rib celery, sliced finely
3   tablespoons margarine
⅛   teaspoon pepper
1   (12 ounce) can evaporated milk
¾-1 cup instant potato flakes

Combine potatoes, water, ¼ teaspoon salt, carrot, onion and celery in a large saucepan. Bring to a boil; cover and reduce heat. Simmer 15 minutes until tender. To this mixture, add margarine, ½ teaspoon salt, pepper, evaporated milk and return to high to boil. Add instant mashed potato flakes, stirring constantly, until soup is slightly thickened. Soup will thicken further as it cools. Choose the desired thickness by careful addition of the potato flakes.

Yield: 6 servings

Taco Soup

1 pound ground beef, cooked and drained	1 (8 ounce) can tomato sauce
¼ cup chopped onion	1 (16 ounce) can kidney beans, not drained
3 cups water	
1 (16 ounce) can stewed tomatoes, coarsely chopped but not drained	1 (4.5 ounce) can chiles, diced
	1 package taco seasoning mix

Cook beef with onion until brown. Add remaining ingredients and simmer 15 minutes. Serve with tortilla chips, cheese and sour cream.

Yield: 8 servings

Every year the Callaway Gardens Education Department participates in a time-honored Christmas tradition — the National Audubon Society's Christmas Bird Count. Started in 1900 by a small group of birdwatchers in the Northeast, this event now includes more than 44,000 participants and more than 1,650 counts in geographic locations from Alaska to Guam.

Microwave Vidalia Onion Soup

¼ pound unsalted butter	Freshly ground pepper
4 cups sliced Vidalia® onions	6 toast slices
2 cups dry white wine	12 tablespoons Gruyère cheese, grated
2 cups chicken broth	
Salt	

Heat butter in 14x12 inch casserole dish, uncovered, in microwave for 4 seconds on high. Add onions; stir to coat with butter. Cook, uncovered, on high 3 to 4 minutes, depending on desired brownness and power of microwave. Stir 3 or 4 times during cooking. Onions will brown unevenly. Add wine and broth. Continue cooking on high for 15 minutes. Meanwhile heat broiler. Remove soup from microwave. Season with salt and pepper. Divide soup into 6 ovenproof bowls. Place piece of toast (cut to fit) on top of each bowl. Sprinkle with 2 tablespoons grated cheese. Place bowls on cookie sheet. Broil 3 minutes or until cheese begins to brown.

Yield: 6 servings

Georgia Peanut Soup

1	medium onion, chopped	2	quarts chicken stock
2	ribs celery, chopped	2	cups creamy peanut butter
¼	cup butter	1¾	cups light cream
3	tablespoons flour		Chopped peanuts

Sauté onion and celery in butter until soft. Blend in flour. Add chicken stock, stirring constantly until smooth. Bring to a boil. Remove from heat and rub through a sieve. Add peanut butter and cream, blending thoroughly. Return to low heat. DO NOT BOIL. Serve hot, garnished with peanuts.

Yield: 12 servings

Black Beans and Rice

1	pound dried black beans	8	cups chicken stock
¼	pound bacon	1	bay leaf
5	garlic cloves, minced	1	tablespoon chili powder
2	ribs celery, minced	1	teaspoon cumin
1	large carrot, diced	1	teaspoon cayenne pepper
1	medium onion, diced	¾	teaspoon white pepper
1	jalapeño pepper, diced	2	pounds Italian sausage,
2	red bell peppers, diced		cooked

Soak beans overnight in enough water to cover, changing water 2 or 3 times. Then boil for 20 minutes in water. Drain and rinse. Fry bacon until crisp and set aside to use as garnish. Sauté vegetables in oil or bacon drippings. Drain. Add vegetables to beans; add broth and spices. Cook several hours until tender and flavorful. Add cooked sausage and heat through just before serving. Serve on a bed of brown rice with green salad and crusty bread. Garnish with chopped onions and crumbled bacon.

Yield: 12 servings

One of our summer guests' favorite memories is riding the train at Robin Lake Beach. The Whistlin' Dixie *chugged around Chickadee Lake for 20 years, carrying children and adults on a memorable excursion through the woods. Due to wear and tear, the* Whistlin' Dixie *eventually had to be taken out of service. However, in response to popular demand, it was put back on track in 1995 as the* Chickadee Choo Choo. *Now, children who rode the original train are bringing their children to share the experience and make childhood memories of their own.*

Vegetable Lentil Soup

2	medium carrots	1	cup lentils
2	ribs celery	2	(14½ ounce) cans chicken broth
1	medium onion		
2	tablespoons canola oil	¾	pound red potatoes
1	(15½ ounce) can stewed tomatoes	3	cups water
		1	head escarole

Peppers are actually fruits because they contain seeds which can become new plants.

Dice carrots, celery and onion. Cook in oil until tender, stirring often. Stir in tomatoes, lentils, broth, diced potatoes and water. Heat to boiling. Reduce heat. Cover and simmer 1 hour. Just before serving, add thinly sliced escarole. Stir until wilted.

Yield: 10 servings

Jimbo's Gumbo

¾	cup vegetable oil	1	bunch fresh parsley, chopped
½	cup real bacon bits		
¾	cup flour	1	(26 ounce) package frozen, sliced okra
4	cubes chicken bouillon		
1	(6 ounce) can tomato paste	2	teaspoons black pepper
8	cups water	2	teaspoons salt, or to taste
2	large onions, chopped	1	teaspoon paprika
1	bell pepper, chopped	2	pounds raw, shelled, cleaned shrimp
4	green onions, chopped		
2	cloves garlic, chopped	½	pound crabmeat
4	ribs celery, chopped		

In a large pot, heat vegetable oil, add bacon bits. Make a roux by stirring flour slowly into the oil, on medium heat, until it is brown. Add bouillon cubes, tomato paste and water. Stir over heat until roux thickens. Have vegetables chopped and ready to place in the mixture along with okra, pepper, salt and paprika. Simmer 2 hours or longer. Fifteen minutes before serving, add shrimp and crab. Serve over rice.

3 tablespoons dried flakes may be substituted for fresh parsley and 2 cans crabmeat may be substituted for fresh crabmeat.

Yield: 12 servings

Pine Bark Stew – A Fish Chowder

½	pound streak-o-lean or slab bacon, chopped	1	tablespoon Worcestershire sauce
2	large onions, chopped		Hot sauce to taste
1	(1 quart 14 ounce) can vegetable juice	1	bay leaf
2	(1 pound) cans stewed tomatoes	2	teaspoons sugar
		1½	pounds fresh, cleaned fish

Sauté streak-o-lean until lightly browned. Remove pieces and reserve. Sauté onions in pork fat until tan. Remove onions to Dutch oven. Add reserved meat bits and all other ingredients except fish. Simmer 30 minutes. Add fish and simmer about 20 minutes, until fish flakes but does not fall apart. Remove and discard bay leaf. Serve over a large hunk of toasted home-made bread in a soup bowl. Accompany with a tart cole slaw.

2 (10 ounce) packages of frozen fish fillets may be used.

Yield: 6 to 8 servings

Southern Catfish Chowder

2	pounds deboned catfish	¼	teaspoon pepper
3	bacon strips	1	green pepper, chopped
1	large onion, chopped	3	potatoes, pared and cubed
1	(15½ ounce) can tomatoes	1	carrot, chopped
1½	teaspoons salt	½	teaspoon vinegar

Cover catfish with water and cook until meat will separate from the bone. Take fish from water and let cool so that it can be handled easily. Save water for chowder. While this is cooling, prepare other ingredients. Cut bacon in 1 inch pieces and fry until brown. Remove from pan; add onion and fry until golden brown. Pour off grease and add tomatoes, salt, pepper, green pepper, potatoes, carrots and bacon. Add about 1 quart of the fish broth. Cook for about 20 minutes or until vegetables are done. Add fish, which has been separated from the bone, and the vinegar. Cook 10 minutes longer. For a thinner chowder, add more broth.

Yield: 6 servings

Americans eat 800 million pounds of peanut butter annually, or 3.3 pounds per person. One 12-ounce jar of peanut butter contains an average of 540 peanuts. One acre of peanuts can yield 30,000 peanut butter sandwiches. A typical high school graduate will have consumed 1,500 peanut butter and jelly sandwiches by graduation day.

Brunswick Stew

1	4 to 6 pound hen	4	tablespoons chicken fat
3	pounds pork shoulder	2	(1 pound) bottles catsup
½	cup chopped onion	2½	ounces Worcestershire
2	cans cream style corn		sauce
2	bread slices	1	tablespoon vinegar
2	cups chicken broth		Red pepper to taste
1	cup pork broth		Salt to taste
1	cup water		Hot sauce to taste

Boil chicken and pork separately until tender. Remove meat. Boil broth to reduce slightly. Remove meat from bones; add onion, corn and bread. Grind. Mix with broth, water, chicken fat and simmer 3 to 4 hours, stirring occasionally. Add catsup, Worcestershire sauce, vinegar, red pepper, salt and hot sauce. Heat to serve.

This freezes well.

Yield: 2 gallons

"Cason Callaway dared venture into leadership in a field despised and forlorn, a field as complex as it was unpopular. In a day when thousands of Americans were fleeing the farm for the city, he fled the city for the farm. Blue Springs became an island of fertility, dramatic, heart-lifting, astounding. There had never been anything like it since the plow first broke West Georgia's virgin soil."
— *from* Cason Callaway of Blue Springs

Letha's Chicken Stew (Cacciatore)

¼	cup olive oil	8	ounces tomato sauce
3	pounds chicken, cut up	1	teaspoon salt
2	medium onions, cut in	¼	teaspoon pepper
	¼ inch slices	¾	teaspoon celery seed
2	cloves garlic, minced	1½	teaspoons oregano
2	cups canned tomatoes	2	bay leaves

Heat oil. Add chicken and brown slowly, turning once. Remove from pan. Cook onions and garlic until tender, but not brown. Add remaining ingredients. Return the chicken to the pan and cook covered about 45 minutes. Do not let sauce bubble or spatter. Cook uncovered 20 minutes or until it reaches the consistency of chili sauce. Drain off excess fat. Serve with noodles or spaghetti. A salad, green vegetable and garlic bread completes the meal.

Yield: 4 servings

Colonel Tom's Brunswick Stew

3	pounds chicken	1	(14 ounce) bottle tomato juice
3	pounds lean pork (fresh, picnic or Boston butt)	1	(14 ounce) bottle catsup
2	large onions	3	pounds corn, canned or frozen
2	teaspoons crushed red pepper	1	(15 ounce) box plain bread crumbs
4	dashes hot sauce		
	Salt and pepper to taste		

Boil chicken in 3 quarts water until meat begins to fall off the bones. Drain, reserving broth in an 8 quart pot. Remove skin. Debone and grind meat on coarse grind. Set aside. Wrap pork in foil. Bake in 325 degree oven for 25 minutes per pound. Remove any fat and bone. Grind on coarse grind. Set aside. Chop onions in food processor or grind very finely. In a large pot, put onions, red pepper, hot sauce, salt, pepper and broth. Bring to a boil. Boil slowly for 30 minutes, covered. Add tomato juice, catsup and meat. Bring to slow boil for 15 minutes, uncovered, stirring often. Add corn, bring back to boil. Boil slowly 15 minutes, stirring to prevent sticking or scorching. Turn off heat. To thicken, add bread crumbs to desired thickness.

This freezes well and tastes even better after freezing.

Yield: 20 servings

Irish Stew

1	pound stewing lamb	2	medium carrots
2	large potatoes, sliced	2	medium onions
	Salt and pepper to taste	1	rib celery
1	teaspoon parsley		

Trim all fat from meat, spread half the sliced potatoes in a cooking pot. Season with salt and pepper. Put meat on top. Sprinkle with chopped parsley, layer onions, carrots and celery. Top with remaining potatoes. Add water to cover. Cook on medium low heat, covered, for 1½ to 2 hours. Skim fat from top.

Chicken or beef may be substituted for lamb.

Yield: 4 servings

Escargot have been a delicacy since prehistoric days. Piles of snail shells have been uncovered in prehistoric sites, indicating they were popular even then. Ancient Romans cultivated special vineyards on which snails could feed and fatten. The vineyard snail is considered the best eating, however the smaller French petitgris is now being cultivated in the United States.

Marion Potts Jones' Christmas Eve Oyster Stew

½ cup cream	1 teaspoon salt
2 cups milk	Fresh ground pepper
¼ cup sweet butter	3 teaspoons Worcestershire
1 pint oysters including liquid	sauce, optional

Heat milk and cream to scalding (150 degrees) in a 2 quart saucepan. Just before serving, in a small saucepan, melt the butter. Add oysters and liquid. Cook gently until oyster edges curl. Overcooking will make them tough. Add to milk and cream. Season with salt and pepper. Add Worcestershire sauce if desired. Pour into cups, dividing evenly. Serve at once. Traditionally, oyster crackers are served with the stew.

Yield: 4 to 6 servings

Old-Time Beef Stew

2 pounds beef chuck, cut into 1½ inch cubes	1 clove garlic (optional)
2 tablespoons vegetable oil	1 bay leaf (optional)
4 cups boiling water	1 dash allspice (optional)
1 tablespoon salt	6 medium carrots, cut into pieces
½ teaspoon black pepper	1 pound small whole potatoes
½ teaspoon paprika	1 pound small white onions
1 tablespoon Worcestershire sauce	

Heat vegetable oil in skillet or stew pot; brown beef cubes on all sides. Add boiling water, salt, pepper, paprika and Worcestershire sauce. (If using garlic, bay leaf and/or allspice, add at this time). Cover and simmer 2 hours, stirring often to keep from sticking. When meat is almost done, add carrots, potatoes and onions. Simmer 30 minutes more or until vegetables are tender. Remove from heat. To thicken, use ½ cup cold water blended with ¼ cup flour. Push meat and vegetables to the side of pan. Add flour mixture and stir until gravy thickens. Mix with meat and vegetables and cook gently for a few minutes. Remove and discard bay leaf before serving.

Yield: 8 servings

Festive Salad Sandwich For Luncheon

Egg Salad for Sandwich

Hard-boiled eggs
Chopped pickle
Mayonnaise

Salt and pepper to taste
Lettuce leaves

Salad

Tomatoes
Boiled shrimp, or lump
   crabmeat, fresh, frozen or
   canned

Olives
Pickled beets

Thousand Island Salad Dressing

1   cup real mayonnaise
2   heaping tablespoons chili
    sauce
1   tablespoon finely chopped
    green pepper

1   tablespoon chopped onion
1   chopped hard-boiled egg
1   tablespoon vinegar

Mix all Egg Salad ingredients, except lettuce. Make sandwich, cut crust off the bread, but do not cut sandwich in half. Place 3 lettuce leaves on a dinner plate. Place sandwich in the middle of the lettuce. Place 1 large slice tomato on top of the sandwich. On top of this, place boiled shrimp or lump crab or a combination of both. Arrange a couple of olives and a pickled beet slice on the side of the plate. Blend Salad Dressing ingredients. Place a small amount of dressing on top of the sandwiches. Pass any remaining dressing to those who wish more. Serve with potato chips. Your guests will be amazed at how good this combination really is and it looks pretty, too!

Yield 1 serving. Prepare as many as needed.

Asparagus Sandwich Spread

1   (15 ounce) can asparagus,
    drained
2   chopped hard-boiled eggs
¼   cup almonds, toasted and
    grated

Grated celery to taste
1   small onion, chopped fine
1   dash red pepper
Mayonnaise to moisten

Mix all ingredients. Spread on fancy shaped bread slices and serve open faced.

Yield: 14 servings

The Cason J. Callaway Memorial Forest is a transitional zone where eastern deciduous and southern coniferous forests mingle. There is a unique diversity of wildlife as well, with species represented from the Appalachian, Piedmont and Coastal Plain regions. The various communities provide excellent habitats for many kinds of mammals including bats, fox squirrels and raccoons; birds such as wild turkeys, pileated woodpeckers and cardinals; reptiles including fence lizards and eastern box turtles; and amphibians such as American toads, green frogs and dusky salamanders.

Hawaiian Sandwiches

1½ cups ground cooked ham	¼ cup mayonnaise
¼ cup chopped cocktail peanuts	1 tablespoon light brown sugar
½ cup crushed pineapple, drained	1 teaspoon prepared mustard

Thoroughly mix together all ingredients. Chill. Spread on your favorite bread and cut for tea sandwiches.

Yield: 1¼ cups

Canadian Croissant Sandwich

½ small avocado	2 large spinach leaves
1 tablespoon cucumber salad dressing	2 thin slices red onion
6 thin slices Canadian bacon	1 whole wheat croissant, split lengthwise

Mash avocado in small bowl. Stir in dressing. To assemble sandwich, layer three slices of bacon, spinach leaves and red onion on top half of croissant. Put remaining bacon on bottom half of croissant. Spoon avocado mixture on top. Close sandwich and enjoy!

Yield: 1 sandwich

Henry Orr's Hot Mustard

5 tablespoons Coleman's® English mustard powder	½ teaspoon salt
2 tablespoons flour	½ cup vinegar
⅓ cup sugar	1 cup milk
	1 egg yolk

Combine dry ingredients. Combine liquid ingredients. Pour liquid ingredients over dry ingredients and mix well. Cook in a saucepan over medium heat, stirring often to prevent burning. Cook until thickened. Remove from heat. Cool before refrigerating. Excellent on ham and turkey sandwiches.

Make sure to use Coleman's® mustard, as other dry mustards do not taste as good.

Henry Orr was an Auburn University Horticulture Professor.

Yield: Approximately 2 cups

The large oil painting of ducks in the flight that hangs in the Gardens Restaurant was painted by Athos Menaboni, a famous wildlife artist who was a close family friend of the Callaways. He painted more than 150 species of American birds using pencil, pastels, oil, water colors and other media. His work is exhibited in major museums worldwide, including the Smithsonian Institution.

Frances Potts' Summertime Cheese Melts

1	slice bread or bun	2	slices crisply fried bacon
1	thick slice vine-ripened tomato	1	slice sharp cheddar cheese
1	thin slice Vidalia® onion		Vegetable cooking spray

Preheat oven to 400 degrees. Lightly butter bread or bun (or spray with vegetable cooking spray). Peel tomato and cut to width of bread. Spray onion on both sides with cooking spray and microwave 30 seconds on high. Assemble by layering tomato on bread or bun, then the onion slice, cover with bacon, top with cheddar cheese and run under broiler until cheese melts. Do this in a large oven on a cookie sheet far enough away from the broiler so that all ingredients are HOT. Serve at once! Use a knife and fork to eat.

Yield: 1 sandwich

Olive Nut Sandwich Spread

1	(8 ounce) package cream cheese, at room temperature	¾	cup chopped pecans
		1	cup chopped green olives
½	cup mayonnaise	2	tablespoons olive juice
			Dash of pepper (no salt)

Mix well. Put in jar and refrigerate 24 to 48 hours until it thickens. Spread on bread for a different and tasty sandwich.

Yield: 4 sandwiches

Raisin-Nut-Pineapple Tea Sandwiches

1	(8 ounce) package cream cheese	1	tablespoon sugar (optional)
1	(8¼ ounce) can crushed pineapple, slightly drained	1	loaf raisin-nut bread

Blend softened cream cheese with crushed pineapple. Add some of the remaining juice to the spread, if needed. If pineapple is unsweetened, add 1 tablespoon sugar. Set aside. Trim edges of bread. Make sandwiches. Cut in desired shapes and sizes.

Yield: 30 to 32 tea size sandwiches

Milestone Openings in Callaway Gardens history:

1952 Gardens opens to public

1953 Robin Lake beach

1960 Mr. Cason's Vegetable Garden

1962 Ida Cason Callaway Memorial Chapel

1984 John A. Sibley Horticultural Center

1988 Cecil B. Day Butterfly Center

1989 Discovery Bicycle Trail

1990 Chapel renovation and dedication

1992 Fantasy In Lights debut

1999 Callaway Brothers Azalea Bowl

2000 Virginia Hand Callaway Discovery Center

Shrimp Salad on Croissant

Shrimp Salad

3 cups cooked shrimp, peeled and chopped	½ cup sliced green onions
1 cup finely chopped celery	3 large hard-boiled eggs, chopped
½ cup sliced olives	

Dressing

¾ cup mayonnaise	¼ teaspoon salt
2 tablespoons chili sauce	8 large croissants, split
2 teaspoons horseradish	

Combine salad ingredients. Combine dressing ingredients, then toss together gently. Fill croissants when ready to serve.

Yield: 8 sandwiches

Be sure to wear rubber gloves when cutting hot peppers, and hold them by the stems. Never touch your face or eyes after handling hot peppers until you have washed your hands thoroughly.

Pimiento Cheese

16 ounces sharp cheddar cheese	3 tablespoons real mayonnaise
1 (8 ounce) jar pimientos, drained and chopped	Salt to taste

Grate cheese by hand. Mix with drained pimentos in a flat dish, such as a pie plate or casserole dish. Mash the mixture using a fork. Add mayonnaise and salt to taste. Mash for about 5 to 10 minutes. If more mayonnaise is needed, add it cautiously. Avoid individual grates of cheese. Mixture should be smooth, but not soupy. Refrigerate overnight. This should make about 16 sandwiches.

Yield: 4 cups

The Hermit (Oceanside Country Club)

2 slices rye bread	¼ cup onion, sautéed
1 thick slice (or 2 thin slices) sharp cheddar cheese	1 tomato, chopped or sliced
	2 slices bacon, crisply fried

Assemble sandwich. Butter each side of bread and grill. Slice in half.

Yield: 1 sandwich

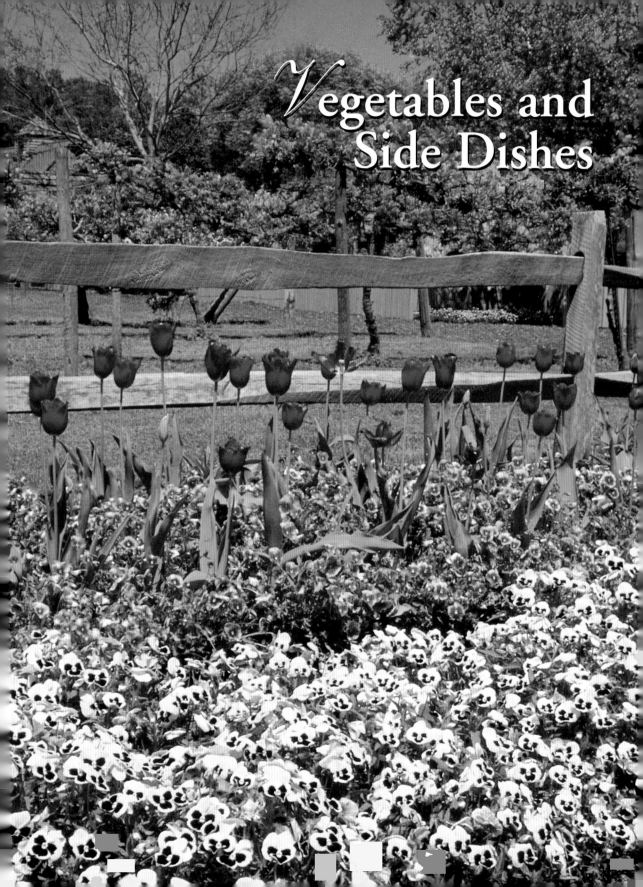

Vegetables and
Side Dishes

Mr. Cason's Vegetable Garden

Everything grows well here . . .

Mr. Cason's Vegetable Garden is an outstanding 7.5 acres of demonstration areas that bring gardening to life. The Vegetable Garden was the last major project initiated by Gardens founder Cason J. Callaway before his death, and it is affectionately named in his memory.

If the garden looks familiar, maybe it's because this is the Southern setting for the popular PBS television show, *The Victory Garden.* Although referred to as the Vegetable Garden, much more than just vegetables grow here. The Vegetable Garden's design includes areas for fruits, herbs, flowers, an All America Trials garden, a composting area and more. But most home gardeners who visit Mr. Cason's Vegetable Garden find that what grows here best is inspiration!

 Callaway Family Recipes

Southern Beets

1	pound fresh beets	3	tablespoons water	
¼	cup sugar	1	small onion, diced	
¼	cup vinegar		Salt and pepper to taste	

Boil beets until tender. Skin, slice and set aside. Combine sugar, vinegar and water. Add beets, onion, salt and pepper. Allow to marinate about 8 hours.

Leaving 1 inch green on both ends of beets before boiling, prevents 'bleeding.'

Yield: 4 servings

Green Beans

4	cups fresh green beans, washed well	2	tablespoons sugar (optional)
1	small piece salt pork or 1 ham hock	2	tablespoons vinegar (optional)
	Salt to taste		

Snap beans. They may be broken into 1 inch pieces or left whole. Put beans and meat in boiler large enough to hold without overflowing. Add just enough water to cover. Bring to a boil; then reduce heat to boil slowly until beans and meat are tender. Remove from liquid and serve.

2 (15¼ ounce) cans green beans may be substituted for fresh beans.

Small potatoes or small yellow squash may be placed on top of beans while cooking, and when tender served along with the beans.

Yield: 6 servings

When root vegetables are roasted, their natural sugars caramelize giving them a sweeter and more robust flavor. To caramelize the sugars, vegetables should be roasted in a hot oven and should be covered for half of the roasting time.

Broccoli Casserole

2	(10 ounce) packages frozen chopped broccoli	½	cup mayonnaise
1	(10¾ ounce) cream of mushroom soup, undiluted	1	heaping teaspoon chopped onion
1	egg, beaten		Salt and pepper to taste
½	cup grated sharp cheddar cheese	1	tube round buttery crackers, crushed
			Butter

Cook broccoli about 5 minutes. Drain well. Mix all other ingredients together, except crackers and butter. Fold in the broccoli and put into a baking dish. Top with cracker crumbs. Dot with butter. Bake at 350 degrees for 45 minutes. Serve hot.

Cook 1 medium head broccoli for 20 minutes; drain and cut into bite size pieces. Mix above listed ingredients, except increase cheese and mayonnaise to 1 cup each, use 2 eggs and eliminate the onion. Fold in broccoli. Mix ½ package herb seasoned stuffing with ¼ quarter stick melted butter for the topping.

Yield: 8 servings

Timbers to build the pavilion and gazebo at the Callaway Brothers Azalea Bowl were imported from California and North Carolina. The stone came from North Carolina and northern Alabama.

Rumble-de-Thumps (Scottish Dish of the Borders)

¼	head cabbage	2	tablespoons margarine
4	potatoes, peeled		Salt and pepper to taste
½	onion, sliced	1	cup shredded sharp cheddar cheese

Slice cabbage and boil until tender. Cook potatoes and onions until medium soft. With mixer, whip potatoes and onions. Season with margarine, salt and pepper. In buttered casserole, layer whipped potatoes. Drain the cooked cabbage and place on top of the potatoes. Sprinkle a scant amount of shredded cheese on this layer. Top with remaining whipped potatoes. Sprinkle top with remaining cheese. Bake, uncovered, at 350 degrees for 30 minutes or until lightly browned on top.

Yield: 6 servings

Skillet Vegetable Side Dish

2	tablespoons olive oil	2	tablespoons Worcestershire
3	carrots, thinly sliced		sauce
1	large onion, chopped	2	tablespoons minced fresh
½	medium head cabbage,		parsley
	chopped	1	teaspoon caraway seed
½	medium green bell pepper,	½	teaspoon celery salt
	chopped	1	teaspoon dried Italian
2	cloves garlic, minced		seasoning

In large skillet, heat oil on medium high heat. Cook and stir carrots, onion, cabbage and green pepper for 15 minutes. Add remaining ingredients. Cook and stir about 5 minutes longer or until the vegetables are done.

Yield: 8 servings

The picturesque arched bridge in the Azalea Bowl is made of treated Douglas Fir and is 100 feet long and almost 11 feet wide.

Sweet and Sour Cabbage

1	small onion, minced	2	apples, peeled, cored and
4	tablespoons butter		grated
2	strips bacon	½	cup raisins
1	small cabbage, cored and	1	cup apple juice
	finely shredded	3	tablespoons sugar
		3	tablespoons lemon juice

Sauté onion in butter until transparent. Slice bacon in ½ inch pieces before cooking. Cook until brown and drain. Place all ingredients in a Dutch oven, cover, lower heat and simmer for about 45 minutes, stirring occasionally until cabbage is tender. Add a little apple juice if necessary to avoid scorching.

Yield: 6 servings

Dijon Cauliflower

1	medium head cauliflower	1	teaspoon Dijon mustard
	Salt and pepper to taste		Cheddar cheese, shredded
½	cup mayonnaise		

Cook cauliflower about 20 minutes. Break into bite size pieces; salt and pepper to taste and place in a 1½ quart casserole. Mix mayonnaise and mustard. Top cauliflower with mustard mixture. Top with shredded cheese. Bake at 350 degrees until cheese is bubbly.

Yield: 6 servings

Celery and Carrot Crunch

1	bunch celery	1¼	teaspoons salt
½	cup onion rings	¼	teaspoon pepper
¼	cup margarine	¼	cup slivered almonds,
1	cup coarsely grated carrots		toasted

Slice celery thin on diagonal to make 6 cups. Stir-fry celery and onions in margarine for 6 to 8 minutes at 300 degrees in electric skillet. Stir in carrots, salt and pepper. Stir-fry for 2 minutes. Add almonds. A colorful and addictive vegetable dish!

Yield: 4 servings

Corn on the Cob

4	ears fresh corn	Salt and pepper to taste
	Butter or margarine,	All-purpose seasoning
	softened	blend

Remove husks from corn. Spread corn generously with butter or margarine and sprinkle with salt, pepper and seasoning blend. Wrap each ear in foil, sealing and twisting foil around ends. Place on grill over hot coals for 15 to 20 minutes or until tender, turning often.

Yield: 4 servings

Hilda Crockett's Corn Pudding

½-1 cup sugar
3 tablespoons cornstarch
2 eggs
1 (16 ounce) can creamed
  corn

1 (13 ounce) can evaporated
  milk
Butter

Preheat oven to 350 degrees. Lightly grease a 1½ quart baking dish. Combine sugar and cornstarch in medium bowl. Add eggs, corn and milk, mixing well. Turn into baking dish and dot generously with butter. Bake until center is almost firm, about 1 hour.

Yield: 8 servings

"Corn Tamale" Casserole

1 (15½ ounce) can whole
  kernel corn
1 (14½ ounce) can tomatoes,
  cut up
1 medium onion, diced
1 green bell pepper, diced
4 tablespoons salad olives

2 eggs, beaten
5 tablespoons yellow corn
  meal
1 cup grated cheese
1 cup milk
1 tablespoon Parmesan
  cheese

Mix all of the vegetables. Add eggs, corn meal, cheese and milk. Pour into greased casserole and sprinkle with Parmesan cheese. Cook in 350 degree oven until firm, approximately 30 minutes.

Yield: 6 servings

The Day Butterfly Center is filled with colorful "flying jewels" and tropical plants. Butterflies have always been fascinating to people. Finnish folklore tells us that the soul leaves the body as a butterfly while a person is asleep, and this accounts for dreams. In the Solomon Islands, people believe that the dead may choose the form they use to return to earth, and many choose to come back as butterflies. When a butterfly dies, it is thought to be the end of the soul forever.

Microwave Creamed Corn

6	ears fresh white corn	2	tablespoons milk
½	stick margarine	1	tablespoon flour, as needed
	Salt and pepper to taste	1	tablespoon milk (if needed)

The cinnamon fern is not used as a spice, but is named for the striking color of its fertile fronds.

Shuck, silk and cut corn off the cob. When cutting from the cob, take the knife and cut lengthwise down the center of each row of niblets. Then slice off the tip (or first layer) of corn. With the back side of knife, scrape the rest of the corn off the cob into a glass microwave proof bowl. This makes a milky liquid with tiny niblets of corn. Cover with plastic wrap or lid. Cook on high in microwave for 7 minutes. Stir. Add ½ stick (or less) margarine. Salt and pepper to taste. Add 2 tablespoons milk. Microwave on high for 3 minutes. If corn seems soupy, mix 1 tablespoon flour in 1 tablespoon milk until the mix is smooth, not lumpy. Add to corn. Microwave on high for 2 minutes. Stir. When thickened, it is ready to serve.

Yield: 8 servings

Country Fresh Corn

6	ears fresh corn	1	teaspoon sugar
3	cups water	1	teaspoon salt
3	tablespoons margarine	⅛	teaspoon pepper

Shuck, remove silks and rinse corn. Combine water and corn in a large saucepan. Bring to a boil, cover, reduce heat and simmer 20 minutes until tender. Remove corn from water. Reserve ⅔ cup water which corn has been cooked in. Using corn cutter or knife, cut tip of grains into saucepan and scrape cob. Combine cut corn, reserved water, margarine, sugar salt and pepper. Bring to a boil, cover, reduce heat and simmer 5 minutes.

DO NOT BOIL CORN. Shuck, silk and cut corn off the cob following above instructions. Fry 4 to 6 slices of bacon in a heavy cast iron skillet until crisp. Remove bacon and set aside. Pour off all but 2 tablespoons bacon drippings and add corn to the skillet. Salt and pepper to taste. Simmer for approximately 20 minutes, stirring frequently to avoid sticking and burning. If necessary add a little water. Serve crumbled bacon on top.

Yield: 6 servings

Southern Turnip Greens

1 large pan filled with turnip greens	1 teaspoon sugar (optional)
1½ quarts water	¼ cup vinegar (optional)
4 ounces lean ham or 2 ham hocks or ½ pound streak-o-lean	Salt to taste

Wash turnip greens well. It may take 3 or 4 washings. Place greens in large boiler. Add water and meat. Boil until tender. Remove from water and cut into very small pieces. Salt to taste. Serve with the pork meat and corn bread.

Since all greens, whether turnip, collards, mustard, rape, beet tops or spinach, cook down considerably, an 8 quart pan is a good size to use.

Yield: 6 servings

The first jack o'lantern was carved out of a turnip in Ireland.

Baked Stuffed Eggplant

1 medium eggplant	1½ teaspoons salt
1 tablespoon olive oil	¼ tablespoon ground black pepper
1 onion, chopped	1 teaspoon chopped fresh basil (or ½ teaspoon dried)
1 green pepper, diced	
¼ pound mushrooms, sliced	
2 tomatoes, chopped	

Wash and dry eggplant; halve lengthwise. Scoop out and dice pulp, leaving enough around the edges to keep the shell rigid. Heat oil; sauté onion, pepper, mushrooms and eggplant for about 10 minutes, stirring frequently. Add tomatoes, salt, pepper and basil and continue cooking for 5 minutes. Stuff shells and bake at 375 degrees for about 20 minutes.

Yield: 4 servings

Collard Greens

1	bunch collard greens		Salt to taste
2	ham hocks or 1 pound	2	teaspoons sugar (optional)
	streak-o-lean or slab bacon	¼	cup vinegar (optional

Wash and remove stems from collard leaves. Break leaves into smaller pieces if desired. Put collards and meat into a large boiler; pour in enough water to fill about ¾ full. Bring to a boil; reduce heat so that collards will continue to boil until tender. Remove from water, cut into very small pieces and add salt to taste. (Meat may have been salty). Serve with the meat and corn bread.

Yield 6 servings

Fried Okra Fritters

1	cup boiled okra	½	teaspoon salt
1	egg, beaten		All-purpose flour
¼	cup milk		Vegetable oil
1	teaspoon baking powder		

Mix okra, egg, milk, baking powder and salt together. Add enough flour to make a firm batter. Drop spoonfuls of batter in skillet with hot oil. Brown on both sides. Drain on paper towels.

Yield: 4 servings

Okra and Tomatoes

2	cups fresh or frozen okra	3	cups fresh or canned tomatoes, cut up
3	tablespoons bacon drippings or margarine	1	teaspoon salt
1	cup diced onions (optional)	2	teaspoons sugar (optional)

Heat bacon drippings or margarine in sauce pan. Add okra and onions with a little water. Cook until almost tender. Add tomatoes and season with salt and sugar. Cook about one hour on low heat.

Yield: 8 servings

Onion Casserole

2	large Vidalia® onions, sliced	1	teaspoon soy sauce
2	tablespoons butter or margarine	8	ounces shredded Swiss cheese
1	(10 ounce) can cream of chicken soup, undiluted	½	loaf French bread
½	cup milk	2	tablespoons butter or margarine, melted

Sauté onions in 1 tablespoon butter in a large skillet until crisp tender. Spoon into an 8x12 inch casserole dish. Combine soup, milk and soy sauce. Mix well. Pour over onion. Sprinkle cheese evenly over sauce. Cut bread into ¾ inch slices. Arrange on top of casserole. Brush bread with butter. Bake at 350 degrees for 30 minutes or until golden brown.

Yield: 8 servings

Vidalia Casserole

2	large Vidalia® onions, thinly sliced	10	ounces Havarti cheese, shredded
2	large red onions, thinly sliced	3	tablespoons margarine, melted
12	green onions, chopped and separated	¾	cup dry white wine
10	ounces bleu cheese, crumbled		Pepper to taste

Separate Vidalia and red onions into rings. Keep onions separated. Alternately layer half Vidalia, red, green onions into a greased 13x9 inch casserole. Sprinkle each layer with pepper. Top with blue cheese. Layer second half Vidalia, red and green onions and sprinkle with pepper. Top with Havarti cheese. Drizzle margarine evenly over cheese. Pour wine over casserole. Cover and bake at 325 degrees 45 minutes. Remove cover and bake additional 15 minutes to brown cheese.

Yield: 10 servings

Vidalia® onions are a Southern specialty grown in Georgia's coastal plain region. These remarkably mild and sweet onions can only be grown in 20 counties where sandy soil and mild climate provide its distinct flavor. Vidalia onions are the official state vegetable of Georgia and are available fresh from late April to mid-July.

Vidalia Onions

5	large Vidalia® onions	Parmesan cheese
½	stick butter or margarine (butter is best)	Bread crumbs

Slice onions and sauté butter or margarine until clear (not brown). Place in layers in casserole dish (layer of onions, layer of Parmesan cheese), until all onions are used. Sprinkle breadcrumbs on top. Bake at 325 degrees for approximately 20 to 25 minutes. Delicious!

Yield: 6 servings

Vidalia-Tomato Pie

6	medium tomatoes, peeled and seeded	½-1	teaspoon garlic powder (adjust to taste)
1	can biscuits (5 biscuits) or 1 deep dish pie shell	1	teaspoon basil Salt and pepper to taste
1	medium Vidalia® onion, finely chopped	8	ounces Monterey Jack cheese
		1	cup mayonnaise

Squeeze juice from tomatoes. Drain in a strainer for 30 minutes. Tear biscuits apart and press thinly in a pie plate to make crust or use a deep dish prepared pie shell. Spread ½ onion and ½ tomatoes on crust. Sprinkle with spices. Top with rest of onion and tomatoes. Mix cheese and mayonnaise and spread on top. Bake at 400 degrees, uncovered, for 45 minutes or until lightly browned.

The most important "to-do" in this recipe is squeezing the juice out of the tomatoes so the pie will not be soggy.

Make 2 pies so you have some cold leftovers for snacks or a light meal!

Yield: 6 to 8 servings

Hopping John

2	cups dried black-eyed peas	2	cups long grain rice
1½	quarts cold water	1	teaspoon pepper
1	pound bacon	1	tablespoon salt
5	cups boiling water		

Combine peas and cold water in large heavy pot with tight fitting lid. Cover and cook over medium heat for 1 hour. Remove cover. Turn heat to high and cook until peas are almost dry. Cut bacon into 1½ inch lengths. Add bacon, boiling water, rice, salt and pepper. Stir. Bring to a boil. Cover, reduce heat and simmer for 25 minutes or until moisture is absorbed and rice is tender. Serve topped with bacon pieces.

Sauté ½ bell pepper, chopped, 1 teaspoon oregano, 1 bay leaf, 1 chopped onion and 3 cloves garlic. Add at the same time as the rice.

Yield: 8 to 10 generous servings

Country Mashed Vegetables

5-6	medium potatoes, peeled and quartered	½	stick margarine
1	medium rutabaga, peeled and quartered	1	(12 ounce) can evaporated milk
2	medium carrots, peeled and quartered	2	tablespoons sour cream
			Salt and pepper to taste

Place all vegetables together in a large pot. Cover with water and bring to a boil. When tender, drain and mash with a mixer, adding margarine, milk, sour cream and salt and pepper to taste. Serve mashed potatoes and vegetables at once. However, they can be kept warm by placing the container in a larger pan of hot water, or put vegetables in a greased casserole and keep in a warm oven.

This recipe has been in one family for centuries and, of course, has been modernized a little, but it is still delicious!

Yield: 8 servings

Walking trails at Callaway Gardens:

Callaway Brothers Azalea Bowl   1.25 total

Holly Trail   .75 mile

Laurel Springs   5 miles

Mountain Creek Trail   2.5 miles

Overlook Azalea Garden   1.5 miles

Rhododendron   .25 miles

Wildflower   .75 miles

Oven Baked New Potatoes

10 new potatoes, slightly
   larger than golf balls
   Garlic salt and herbs of
   choice, to taste

No stick cooking spray for
fat free cooking

Scrub and dry potatoes. Quarter and place on cookie sheet or shallow pan. Spray with cooking spray, coating all sides. Sprinkle liberally with garlic salt and any other herb such as dill and/or Parmesan cheese. Bake at 350 degrees stirring often to brown, approximately 45 minutes. Bake as many potatoes as the pan allows.

Yield: 6 servings

For a splendid view of pine-covered mountains, a visit to Callaway Gardens' Country Kitchen is a must. The rustic setting, homey atmosphere and Southern hospitality fit perfectly with the "down-home" country-style cooking. And the view is almost as good as the food!

Roasted Rosemary Potatoes

24 small red potatoes
   (approximately 2 pounds)
1 tablespoon olive oil
   Vegetable cooking spray

1¼ teaspoons whole rosemary,
   crushed
¼ teaspoon dried whole thyme
¼ teaspoon salt
⅛ teaspoon pepper

Scrub potatoes, cut in half and brush with olive oil. Place potato halves skin side down in a single layer on a baking sheet coated with cooking spray. Combine rosemary, thyme, salt and pepper. Sprinkle evenly over potato halves. Bake at 375 degrees for 55 to 60 minutes, or until tender and lightly browned.

Yield: 6 servings

Scalloped Sweet Potatoes and Apples

2	cups sweet potatoes, boiled and sliced	4	tablespoons butter
2	cups sliced apples	½	cup brown sugar
½	cup raisins	1	teaspoon cinnamon
		½	cup water

Put half the potatoes in a 2 quart baking dish, then half the apples. Cover with raisins and 2 tablespoons of butter. Sprinkle with half the sugar and cinnamon. Repeat with the remaining potatoes, apples, raisins, butter, sugar and cinnamon. Pour ½ cup water over mixture. Bake in 350 degree oven, uncovered, for 1 hour.

Yield: 4 servings

Sweet potatoes are a vegetable of the morning glory family.

Potato Pancakes

1	cup complete pancake mix	1	small onion, finely chopped
1	medium potato, peeled and finely chopped or coarsely shredded	¼	teaspoon salt
		1	dash pepper

Prepare pancake mix according to package instructions. Stir in potato, onion, salt and pepper. Spoon batter onto hot, lightly greased griddle and cook on both sides until done.

Yield: 6 servings

Senator Russell's Sweet Potatoes

3	cups sweet potatoes, cooked and mashed	2	eggs
1	cup sugar	1	tablespoon vanilla
		½	cup butter

Topping

1	cup brown sugar, packed	1	cup chopped pecans
⅓	cup flour	⅓	cup butter, softened

Combine potatoes, sugar, eggs, vanilla and butter. Beat with electric mixer for 2 minutes. Pour into a buttered casserole. Mix topping ingredients with a fork and sprinkle on top of potatoes. Bake at 350 degrees for 30 minutes. May prepare in advance.

If doubled, use a 9x13 inch casserole dish to feed 10 people.

Yield: 4 to 6 servings

Dining is at its finest at Callaway Gardens' Georgia Room. This elegant restaurant features a menu of fine new Southern cuisine and exquisite service that makes dining here a tantamount experience. Although a favorite for celebrating special occasions, the Georgia Room makes any day memorable.

Spinach and Artichoke Casserole

1	(14 ounce) can artichoke hearts	2	(3 ounce) packages cream cheese
2	(10 ounce) packages frozen chopped spinach	1	(3 ounce) can French fried onion rings
¾	stick margarine, divided	⅔	cup cracker crumbs
2	(10 ounce) cans cream of mushroom soup		

Drain artichokes and place on bottom of casserole dish, set aside. Cook spinach according to package directions, drain well and mix with ½ stick margarine. Warm mushroom soup with cheese, until cheese melts. (May soften cheese in microwave first). Stir into spinach. Crush onion rings and mix into spinach. Pour over artichokes. Mix ¼ stick margarine, melted, with cracker crumbs and sprinkle on top. Bake at 350 degrees 30 to 40 minutes.

Yield: 10 servings

Spinach and Linguine Casserole

1	(10 ounce) package frozen chopped spinach	2	teaspoons dried onion
1	large egg, beaten	½	teaspoon salt
½	cup sour cream	⅛	teaspoon pepper
¼	cup milk	8	ounces Monterey Jack cheese
6	tablespoons grated Parmesan cheese, divided	4	ounces linguine, cooked and drained

Cook spinach according to package instructions. Drain well. Combine next 8 ingredients, using 3 tablespoons Parmesan cheese and mix well. Stir in spinach and linguine. Turn into a 10x6 inch casserole dish. Sprinkle with 3 tablespoons Parmesan cheese. Bake covered for 15 minutes. Uncover and bake 20 minutes longer.

Yield: 4 servings

Spinach-Topped Tomatoes

1	(10 ounce) package frozen chopped spinach	½	cup chopped onion
2	chicken bouillon cubes	½	cup margarine, melted
	Salt to taste	1	egg, beaten
3	large tomatoes, halved	1	clove garlic
1	cup soft bread crumbs	⅛	teaspoon cayenne pepper
½	cup grated Parmesan cheese	¼	teaspoon pepper
			Shredded Parmesan cheese (optional)

Cook spinach with bouillon in saucepan according to directions. Drain well. Cool slightly. Press out excess liquid. Lightly salt tomato halves. Place cut side down on paper towel for 15 minutes to absorb excess moisture. In a small bowl, combine spinach, cheese, onion, margarine, egg, garlic and peppers. Mix well. Place tomato halves, cut side up in shallow baking dish. Spoon spinach mixture over tomatoes. Sprinkle with cheese. Bake at 350 degrees for 15 minutes.

Yield: 6 servings

The most popular meal at Callaway Gardens is the Friday Night Seafood Buffet in the Plantation Room restaurant.
The Plantation Room has long been known for its delicious and generous buffets laden with mouth-watering selections. Each buffet meal includes the temptations of the dessert buffet. Fresh cheesecakes, brownies, cobblers, puddings, cakes and more provide a sweet ending to every buffet meal.

Carlye Bell's Yellow Squash Casserole

2	pounds yellow squash, sliced	¼-½	cup half-and-half
1	large mild onion, chopped	2	eggs, well beaten
1	teaspoon sugar	1	cup sharp cheddar cheese, finely grated
1	stick butter	¼	cup cracker meal
	Salt and pepper to taste		

The Gardens' Veranda Restaurant is perhaps one of dining's best kept secrets. Tucked away in the lower level of the original club house, this restaurant offers Italian cuisine in a delightfully cozy setting. The menu is a tasty selection of authentic Italian dishes that make you feel as if you're in Italy!

Cook together the squash, onion and sugar. When squash is tender, drain thoroughly and mash. Add all other ingredients, mixing thoroughly. Pour into a buttered 8 inch square casserole dish and bake at 350 degrees for up to 45 minutes, depending on desired firmness.

For a soufflé, separate the eggs, saving out the whites. Beat whites until stiff, fold into mixture and bake at 400 degrees for 20 to 25 minutes. It should be puffy and lightly browned.

Yield: 8 servings

Zucchini Fritatta

4	medium zucchini, grated into strips	2	cups mozzarella cheese, grated
5	large eggs		Nutmeg to taste
			Salt and pepper to taste

Grease bottom of pie pan. In a large bowl, beat eggs and add grated zucchini. Add a few dashes of nutmeg, salt and pepper. Mix together and pour into pie plate. Top with grated mozzarella. Bake at 350 degrees 25 minutes.

Yield: 6 servings

❈ *Bernice's Squash Casserole*

2	cups squash, cooked	¼	stick margarine
1	large yellow onion, chopped		Dash nutmeg
	Salt and pepper to taste	4	round buttery crackers, crushed
3	eggs, separated	1	tablespoon sugar
1	cup heavy white sauce		

White Sauce

3	tablespoons butter or margarine	½	teaspoon salt
3	tablespoons flour	1	cup milk

Cook squash with chopped onion, salt and pepper, until tender. Add egg yolks, then white sauce, margarine, nutmeg, crackers and sugar. Mix together well and fold in beaten egg whites. Grease 1½ quart casserole dish with margarine and sprinkle additional crushed crackers on bottom. Pour squash mixture into casserole dish. Put into a pan of water and bake at 375 degrees for 45 minutes to one hour or until brown. To prepare white sauce, melt butter or margarine. Add flour and salt. Mix well, making a smooth paste. Add milk gradually to butter-flour mixture, stirring constantly. Cook until thick, stirring to prevent lumping.

Yield: 6 servings

The Pine Mountain Ridge near Callaway Gardens is composed of a hard, metamorphic rock called Hollis Quartzite. Such a strong base is the reason the Pine Mountain Ridge did not erode over the centuries into the valleys that surround it now. There is a profusion of mountain springs in this area because of the natural artesian pressure beneath the fractured quartzite bedrock.

Oven Fried Green Tomatoes

½	cup cornmeal	1	tablespoon water
½	teaspoon salt	3	medium green tomatoes, cut in ¼ inch slices
¼	teaspoon pepper		Vegetable cooking spray
1	egg		

Combine cornmeal, salt and pepper and set aside. Combine egg and water and beat well. Dip tomatoes in egg mixture; dredge in cornmeal mixture. Lightly coat a 14x10 inch baking pan with cooking spray. Place tomatoes in a single layer in pan. Bake at 450 degrees for 30 to 40 minutes or until golden brown.

Yield: 6 servings

Tomato Casserole

1¼ cups packaged onion and garlic croutons	2 tablespoons basil
3 medium ripe tomatoes, sliced ½ inch thick	1 tablespoon chives
	Black pepper to taste
6 ounces mozzarella cheese, thinly sliced	4 tablespoon oil
	4 tablespoons vinegar

Place croutons in bottom of 9 inch glass pie plate. Overlap tomatoes and cheese in a circle to cover croutons. Sprinkle with basil, chives and pepper. Microwave on high for 3 minutes. Pour oil and vinegar over top of casserole. Microwave 1 to 2 minutes longer.

Yield: 6 servings

Sherried Fruits

2 tablespoons flour	1 (15¼ ounce) can pineapple, drained
½ cup brown sugar	
1 stick butter	1 (15 ounce) can apricots, drained
1 cup sherry wine	
1 (15 ounce) can pears, drained	1 (14.5 ounce) jar sliced apple rings, drained
1 (15 ounce) can peaches, drained	

Mix flour, sugar, butter and sherry and cook in double boiler until very thick. While hot, pour over drained fruit. Heat in casserole dish in a 350 degree oven for 25 minutes.

Yield: 12 servings

Pineapple Gratin

1   (20 ounce) can pineapple
    chunks or tidbits
⅓   cup sugar
3   tablespoons all-purpose flour
1   cup sharp cheddar cheese,
    shredded

½   cup round buttery cracker
    crumbs
2   tablespoons butter or
    margarine, melted

Drain pineapple, reserving 3 tablespoons juice. Combine reserved juice, sugar and flour. Stir in pineapple and cheese. Spoon into a lightly greased, shallow 2 cup baking dish. Combine cracker crumbs and butter, sprinkle evenly over pineapple mixture. Bake at 350 degrees for 25 minutes or until bubbly. Serve as an accompaniment to turkey, ham, pork or chicken.

Yield: 9 servings

*Spanish moss is
not a moss at all,
but rather a member
of the pineapple family.*

Company Wild Rice

1   cup wild rice
3   cups boiling water
¾   teaspoon salt
2   tablespoons margarine or
    butter
4   tablespoons minced onion
2   tablespoons diced green bell
    pepper
1   (4 ounce) can sliced mush-
    rooms, drained

1   (10½ ounce) can cream of
    mushroom soup
1   cup heavy cream
¼   teaspoon dried marjoram
⅛   teaspoon dried tarragon
1   teaspoon curry powder
¼   teaspoon salt
⅛   teaspoon pepper

Wash rice well 3 or 4 times in cold water, drain. Add salt to boiling water in saucepan and stir in rice. Simmer, covered, 30 to 45 minutes until rice is tender and water is absorbed. While rice cooks, sauté onion, pepper and mushrooms 5 minutes. Stir in soup, cream and spices. Heat 10 minutes. Add rice to this mixture and heat, stirring occasionally. May be combined, placed in a casserole and heated in the oven at 325 degrees for 25 minutes.

A very nice accompaniment to dove or quail.

Yield: 6 to 8 servings

Cornbread Dressing and Gravy

Dressing

1	recipe egg bread	
8	medium biscuits or 8 slices white bread	
6	saltine crackers	
6	large eggs, beaten	
1	stick margarine, melted	
1	cup chopped onion	

Chopped celery to taste
(2 to 3 ribs)
1 (10¾ ounce) can cream of chicken soup, undiluted
Chicken or turkey broth
Black pepper to taste

Gravy

2 cups chicken or turkey broth
½ cup cream of celery, mushroom, or chicken soup, undiluted
1 medium egg, boiled and minced

Cornstarch (or 3 table-spoons uncooked cornbread dressing) to thicken

Crumble bread, biscuits and saltines into a large bowl. Add eggs and butter, mixing well. Add onions, celery and soup. Add pepper and enough broth to make a soft mixture. Pour into a greased 9x13 inch baking dish and bake at 400 degrees until done (about 30 minutes). Prepare gravy by mixing broth, soup and egg. Cook until it begins to thicken. Add cornstarch or uncooked dressing while gravy is slowly boiling.

Cornbread Dressing and Gravy is traditionally served in the South with turkey or chicken.

Yield: 9 servings

Herbed Zucchini Quiche

4	cups zucchini, thinly sliced	½	teaspoon pepper
1	cup chopped onions	1	clove garlic
2	tablespoons margarine	2	well beaten eggs
1	tablespoon fresh basil leaves	2	cups Muenster cheese, shredded
1	tablespoon fresh oregano	1	10 inch prepared pie crust
½	cup fresh, snipped parsley	2	teaspoon prepared mustard
½	teaspoon salt		

Heat oven to 375 degrees. Cook zucchini and onions with margarine in a large skillet about 8 minutes until tender. Stir in basil, oregano, parsley, salt, pepper and garlic. In a large bowl combine eggs and cheese, mixing well. Stir in cooked vegetable mixture. Spread prepared piecrust with mustard. Pour egg/vegetable mixture evenly into crust. Bake at 375 degrees for 18 to 20 minutes or until knife inserted in center comes out clean. Let stand 10 minutes before serving.

Use fresh herbs if possible; however, ¼ teaspoon basil and oregano and 2 tablespoons dried parsley may substitute for fresh.

Yield: 6 servings

Callaway Gardens' Mountain Creek Lake Trail is an unpaved woodland trail along the water's edge. Hikers enjoy diverse flora and fauna and are able to see the interaction of water life with the community at the edge of a forest. Turtles, fish, ducks, heron and other water residents are commonly visible to hikers.

Cumin Rice

2	tablespoons bacon drippings or margarine	2	tablespoons Worcestershire sauce
¼	cup chopped onion	2	cans beef consommé
1¼	cups long grain rice	1	teaspoon cumin seed
			Salt and pepper to taste

Heat drippings or margarine. Add onions and sauté until clear. Add rice, mixing with onions and stirring 3 to 5 minutes. Add Worcestershire sauce, mixing thoroughly. Then add consommé, cumin seed, salt and pepper. Bring to a gentle boil and cook, covered, for 20 to 25 minutes. Do not cook until dry. A small jar of sliced mushrooms may be mixed with the consommé for added interest.

Yield: 6 servings

Rice with Apricots and Pine Nuts

3 tablespoons butter	1 (14½ ounce) can chicken broth
¼ cup pine nuts or almonds	½ cup apricots
1 cup rice	½ cup sliced green onions

Melt butter in a large skillet. Add pine nuts and cook 2 minutes. Remove nuts with slotted spoon. Set aside. Add rice and stir 3 to 5 minutes. Stir in broth and bring to a boil. Simmer 20 minutes. Add nuts, apricots and onions. Cook, covered, 5 minutes longer.

Yield: 6 servings

Cason Callaway grew two varieties of blueberries: Florida high bush and New Jersey true-blue. Agricultural experts insisted New Jersey true-blues could not be grown in Georgia. Managing once again to prove the impossible, Cason planted 600 bushes and all thrived.

Surprise Dressing

2 cups leftover cornbread, crumbled	¾ cup chopped celery
	4 eggs
½ cup dry bread crumbs	½ teaspoon sage
3 cups chicken or turkey broth	½ teaspoon basil
	⅛ teaspoon pepper
½ cup margarine, melted	1 teaspoon salt
¾ cup finely chopped onion	3 hard boiled eggs, halved

Preheat oven to 350 degrees. Combine all ingredients except hard boiled eggs. Mix well. Put a shallow layer of mixture in greased 13x9 inch casserole dish. Place egg halves on top. Cover with remaining dressing. Bake at 350 degrees for 45 to 60 minutes or until lightly browned. Serve with mushroom or giblet gravy.

:Yield: 20 servings

Mustard Mousse

4	eggs	¼	teaspoon salt
¾	cup sugar	1	cup water
1	envelope unflavored gelatin	½	cup cider vinegar
1	tablespoon dry mustard	½	pint whipping cream
½	teaspoon turmeric		

Beat eggs in top of double boiler. Mix sugar and gelatin; stir in mustard, turmeric and salt. Add water and vinegar to the eggs. Stir in the sugar mixture and cook over boiling water until slightly thickened, stirring constantly. Cool until thick. Whip cream and stir in. Turn into a 1½ quart ring mold. When firm, unmold and, if desired, fill center with cole slaw enhanced with frozen or canned pineapple chunks or diced winter pears. Garnish with chicory, watercress or other feathery greens. Serve with roast pork, ham or turkey.

Yield: 8 servings

Cason Callaway's experiments with blueberries led to a superior variety of blueberry eventually being developed in 1940 by the U. S. Department of Agriculture. The berry was named the "Callaway Blueberry" in honor of Cason's work.

Fresh Chopped Tomato Salsa

1½	cups chopped tomatoes	1	teaspoon lemon juice
1	teaspoon salt	½	cup olive oil
1	tablespoon chopped fresh basil	2	tablespoons chopped parsley
1	garlic clove		Fresh cracked black pepper

Chop unpeeled tomatoes in food processor. Leave large, coarse pieces. Drain for 1 hour. Add remaining ingredients and toss.

Yield: Approximately 1½ cups

Pear Relish

15	large pears	5	large onions
5	green peppers	5	cups vinegar
5	red peppers	5	cups sugar
3	hot peppers	1	tablespoons salt

Peel and core pears. Grind pears through coarse food chopper. Drain pears until excess juice is removed. Grind peppers and onions. Combine all ingredients. Bring to a boil and cook for 20 minutes. Fill hot sterilized canning jars with hot mixture, leaving ½ inch headspace. Remove air bubbles. Wipe jar rims. Adjust sterilized lids. Process in hot water bath for 10 minutes. Very good with vegetables, such as butter beans or black-eyed peas as well as meats.

Yield: 10 pints

*Callaway Gardens'
preserve plant was
opened in the 1960s
to process fruit from
our orchard. Today,
its two large steam-
heated cookers
can produce up to
3,000 20-ounce
jars per day.*

Corn Relish

2	(17 ounce) cans whole kernel corn, drained	2	tablespoons vegetable oil
1	(4 ounce) jar pimento, diced and drained	½	cup vinegar
		¼	teaspoon celery seed
1	small sweet red pepper, chopped (optional)	2	teaspoons instant minced onion
½	cup sugar	⅛	teaspoon salt

Combine first 3 ingredients, stirring well. Combine sugar and remaining ingredients in a small saucepan. Bring to a boil; cover, reduce heat and simmer 1 minute. Pour over vegetables and toss gently. Cover and chill at least 2 hours.

Yield: 4 cups

Cranberry Relish

1 cup cranberries	⅓ cup sugar
1 orange	

Wash berries, remove stems and discard soft ones. Remove seeds from orange. Put berries and orange through food chopper or coarse grinder. Add sugar, mix and let stand several hours.

Yield: 2 cups

Pear Chutney

4 pounds sugar	¼ teaspoon red pepper
1 quart vinegar	¼ teaspoon powdered ginger
5 pounds pears, peeled and chopped	1 cup currants
4 green peppers, diced	1 cup crystallized ginger, slivered
4 red peppers, diced	1½ cups slivered almonds
2 large garlic cloves, chopped fine	

Heat sugar and vinegar until sugar dissolves. Add all ingredients. Cook slowly until mixture begins to gel. Pour hot chutney into hot sterilized canning jars leaving ½ inch headspace. Remove air bubbles. Wipe jar rims. Adjust sterilized lids. Process 10 minutes in a boiling water bath.

Yield: 6 pints

Callaway Ginger is a signature plant of Callaway Gardens. It was discovered by Fred Galle, former director of horticulture at Callaway Gardens. It is rarely found in the wild and is one of Georgia's protected plants. It can be seen along the Gardens' Wildflower Trail and is especially noticeable in Winter.

Mango Chutney

4	pounds sugar	½	pound currants or white raisins
1	quart vinegar		
5	pounds mangos, peeled and chopped	2	large garlic cloves
		1	cup crystallized ginger, slivered
4	green bell peppers, sliced thin		
4	red bell peppers, sliced thin	¼	teaspoon red pepper
½	pound slivered almonds	¼	teaspoon powdered ginger

Heat sugar and vinegar until dissolved. Add other ingredients. Cook slowly for 45 minutes. Fill hot sterilized canning jars and follow above directions for processing.

Yield: 4 to 6 pints

Cashews, pistachios and mangos are all relatives of poison ivy.

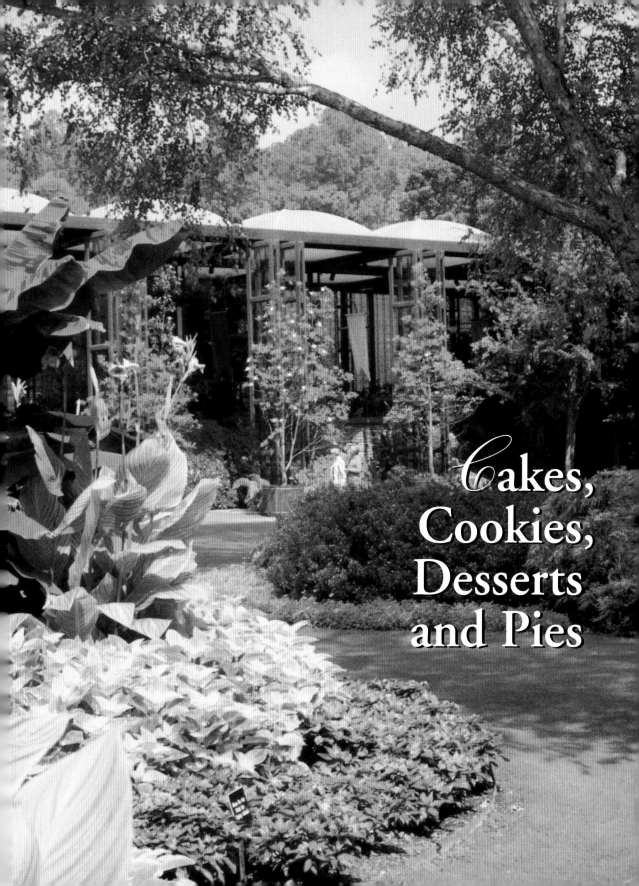

Cakes,
Cookies,
Desserts
and Pies

John A. Sibley Horticultural Center

It's the perfect garden …

…because something's always in bloom at the John A. Sibley Horticultural Center. This one-of-a-kind garden/ greenhouse complex includes five acres of native and exotic plants within its tropical conservatory, rock wall garden, sculpture garden, fern grotto, floral conservatory and outdoor garden. An exhilarating 22-foot indoor waterfall, "Partners in Time" bronze sculpture and special seasonal displays make every visit special. The Sibley Center has come to be known for its endearing Summer topiary shows and enchanting Christmas displays. Nearby production greenhouses provide the beginnings of the beauty that eventually makes the scene at the Sibley Horticultural Center.

Named in memory of John A. Sibley, a Georgia banker, lawyer, civic leader, agricultural enthusiast and friend of the Callaway family, the Center was built on innovative energy-conscious concepts.

The Sibley Center includes a gift shop in the lobby that offers a terrific selection of gardening-themed items including books, tools, birdhouses, T-shirts, toys and home decor items to inspire anyone's green thumb!

 *Callaway Family Recipes*

Banana Cake

Cake

2 eggs	¾ cup milk
1½ cups sugar	2¼ cups self-rising flour
½ cup shortening	½ teaspoon soda
½ cup chopped pecans	1 cup very, very ripe mashed
1 teaspoon vanilla	bananas

Icing

1 very ripe banana	1 box confectioners' sugar
½ teaspoon lemon juice	¼ cup chopped pecans
1 stick margarine, softened	13 pecan halves (optional)
1 teaspoon vanilla	

With mixer, mix ingredients in order that they are listed. Bake in 3 greased 8 inch round cake pans at 350 degrees for 20 minutes or until done. Prepare icing by mashing banana with lemon juice. With mixer, mix mashed banana with soft margarine. Add flavoring. Slowly add the confectioners' sugar. If too thick to spread on cake, use a tiny amount of milk until it is the consistency to spread on the layers. Ice cake. Sprinkle pecans on top of cake. Decorate with pecan halves on top of cake.

This cake is best made two days before serving.

Yield: 16 servings

Thousands of couples have been married in the Ida Cason Callaway Memorial Chapel. In planning the chapel, Cason Callaway imagined the beautiful brides that would choose this idyllic setting for their weddings.

Mama Cannon's Lane Cake

Cake

3¼ cups sifted cake flour	1 cup milk
2 teaspoons baking powder	8 egg whites
1 cup butter	1 teaspoon vanilla
2 cups sugar	

Filling

8 egg yolks	1 cup pecans, chopped fine
1 cup sugar	¾ cup brandy
½ cup butter	1 teaspoon vanilla
1 cup seeded raisins, chopped fine	

Sift flour and baking powder together 3 times. Cream butter and sugar until light. Add to it, alternately a little at a time, milk and flour; beginning and ending with flour. Last, beat in well whipped egg whites and vanilla. Divide batter equally into 3 greased and floured 8 inch round cake pans. Bake at 350 degrees 25 to 30 minutes. To prepare filling, beat well together egg yolks, sugar and butter. Pour into a double boiler and cook over simmering water until quite thick, stirring constantly. When done and still hot, put in raisins, pecans, brandy and vanilla. When cool, spread thickly between layers, side and top.

This cake is best prepared several days before serving.

Yield: 16 servings

One of many medicinal plants used by our forefathers, Oswego Tea was used for curing fevers and relieving stomach aches. Settlers used the leaves to make a tasty mint tea. This member of the mint family is also known as Bee-balm, although the main pollinators are hummingbirds and butterflies.

Nannie's Carrot Cake

Cake

2	cups sugar	2	cups flour, sifted
4	whole eggs	3	teaspoons cinnamon
1½	cups vegetable oil	3	cups grated carrots
2	teaspoons baking soda	2	teaspoons vanilla
1	teaspoon salt		

Cream Cheese Icing

1	stick butter or margarine	1	cup dry-roasted pecans, chopped
8	ounces cream cheese	1	teaspoon vanilla
1	pound powdered sugar, sifted		Pinch of salt

Cream sugar and eggs. Blend in oil. Sift dry ingredients. Add to creamed mixture and blend well. Add vanilla and fold in carrots. Bake in 3 greased 8 inch round cake pans at 325 degrees for 35 to 40 minutes. Cool. To prepare icing, soften butter and cream cheese. Add other ingredients. Blend well and ice cooled cake.

Yield: 12 servings

About a dozen species of bats are residents of the area around Pine Mountain, Georgia. At Callaway Gardens, bat houses are placed in various spots as daytime roosts for Big Brown Bats and Little Brown Bats. These unique flying mammals are harmless and extremely beneficial. One insect-eating bat may feast on up to 3,000 mosquitoes in one night!

Yellow Cake with Orange Icing

Cake

2½	cups flour, sifted	1¼	cups milk
1⅔	cups sugar	3½	teaspoons baking powder
⅔	cups canola oil	3	eggs
½	teaspoon salt	1	teaspoon vanilla

Orange Icing

2	cups applesauce		Juice and rind of one orange
1½	cups sugar		

Mix together first 4 ingredients with ¾ cup milk. Beat for 2 minutes. Stir in ½ cup milk and remaining ingredients. Beat for 2 minutes more. Pour into greased and floured 9 inch tube or Bundt pan. Bake at 375 degrees 30 to 35 minutes. Prepare Orange icing by cooking applesauce, sugar, orange juice and rind on low heat until clear. Pour over top and sides of cake.

Bake in two 8 inch cake pans. Spread icing between each layer.

Yield: 12 servings

Dried Apple Fruit Cake

Cake

2	cups light brown sugar	1	cup chopped nuts (prefer-
¾	cup butter		ably black walnut)
2	large eggs	2	cups raisins
2½	cups dried apples, cooked	1	teaspoon ground nutmeg
	and drained	1	teaspoon ground cloves
4	teaspoons soda	1	teaspoon ground allspice
4	cups all-purpose flour		

Caramel Frosting

3	cups white sugar	1	cup whole milk
1	cup butter		

Cream sugar and butter. Add beaten eggs. Add apples mixed with soda. Add flour mixed with nuts and raisins. Add spices and mix well. Pour into 3 round 8 inch cake pans. Bake at 350 degrees for 30 minutes or until cake layers spring back up when lightly touched. To make caramel frosting, combine sugar and butter and place in a heavy skillet. Place over medium heat and stir until melted. Cook until lightly browned, stirring all the time. Add milk and cook to a soft ball stage. Let cool and beat until thick enough to spread on cake layers.

If apples are sour, add ½ cup sugar to them before adding to batter.

Yield: 20 servings

Allspice is actually one spice derived from the unripened buds of an evergreen tree. Depending on its origin, it may taste like cloves or bay rum. Not only does it add its own flavor to dishes, but it enhances other spices.

Basic Cake Layers (1-2-3-4)

1	cup butter	3	cups all-purpose flour
2	cups sugar	½	teaspoon salt
4	large eggs	1	cup milk
1	teaspoon vanilla		

Cream butter until light. Add sugar and beat until fluffy. Add eggs, one at a time, beating constantly. Add vanilla. Sift together flour and salt. Add alternately with milk to the batter, beginning and ending with flour. Pour batter into 3 lightly greased and floured 9 inch cake pans (or line bottoms of cake pans with waxed paper). Bake at 350 degrees for 20 to 25 minutes. Cool on racks and frost as desired.

Yield: 16 servings

Cocoa and Cola Cake

Cake

1	cup butter, softened	1	teaspoon vanilla
2	cups cake flour	2	eggs
1¾	cups sugar	½	cup buttermilk
3	tablespoons cocoa	1	cup cola
1	teaspoon baking soda	1½	cups miniature marshmallows

Icing

½	cup butter, softened	3	cups powdered sugar
3	tablespoons cocoa	1	cup chopped, toasted pecans (optional)
⅓	cup cola		

Combine all ingredients except cola and marshmallows. Mix well with mixer. Stir in cola and marshmallows (do not use mixer). Bake in 9x13 inch greased and floured pan or casserole dish at 350 degrees for 40 to 45 minutes. Cool. Combine all icing ingredients and mix well. Stir in nuts if desired and spread on cake. Cut into squares to serve.

Classic Coke™ and Pepsi™ have both been suggested for this excellent cake.

Yield: 12 servings

If you have an herb garden or just a little patch of parsley or dill, you may discover greenish worms with yellow and black markings. These parsley worms are actually Black Swallowtail butterflies in the making. These caterpillars actually eat until they pop out of their skin! After doing this about four times, the caterpillar attaches to a stem where it molts one final time to form the chrysalis. In a few weeks an adult butterfly emerges from the chrysalis!

Chocolate Truffle Cake

Crust

1	cup pecans, toasted and ground	¼	cup butter, melted
1	cup graham cracker crumbs	2	tablespoons sugar

Cake

2	(8 ounce) packages semi-sweet chocolate, cut up	6	eggs, beaten
1	cup whipping cream	¾	cup granulated sugar
		⅓	cup all-purpose flour

Combine pecans, crumbs, butter and sugar and press into bottom and about 1½ inches up the sides of a greased 9 inch spring form pan. Set aside. In a large saucepan, cook and stir chocolate and cream over low heat until chocolate melts. Set aside. In a large mixing bowl, combine eggs, sugar and flour; beat 10 minutes or until thick and lemon colored. Fold ¼ of egg mixture into chocolate mix. Fold chocolate mixture into remaining egg mixture. Pour into crust lined pan. Bake in 325 degree oven approximately 45 minutes or until puffed around the edge and halfway to the center (center will be slightly soft). Cool in pan on wire rack for 20 minutes. Remove sides of pan. Cool for 4 hours. If desired, serve with whipped cream. Cover and store in the refrigerator.

Decadently rich!!! And so easy to prepare!!

Yield 16 servings

Visit Callaway Gardens during the winter months and you may spy some buffleheads. These are small ducks with large rounded heads. The males have a white wedge at the back of their head, and females have a long white band behind the eyes. These ducks dive underwater in search of small mollusks, fish, snails, aquatic insects and crustaceans.

Cheesecake Surprise!

Crust

⅔ cup all-purpose flour
2   tablespoons sugar
¼   teaspoon salt

6   tablespoons butter
1   egg yolk, beaten

Filling

1   (8 ounce) package cream
     cheese
⅔ cup sugar
1   tablespoon all-purpose flour
1   teaspoon vanilla

4   eggs
1   egg white
2   cups fresh pears, pared and
     diced

Topping

½   cup fudge topping
1   cup sour cream

⅓ cup powdered sugar
½   teaspoon vanilla

To prepare crust, sift together the flour, sugar and salt. Cut in butter until crumbly; stir in egg yolk, blend in well. Press into 9 inch spring form pan. Bake at 350 degrees for 15 minutes. Cool. Reduce oven temperature to 325 degrees. Prepare filling by beating cream cheese, sugar and flour. Add vanilla. Beat in eggs and egg white. Stir in pears. Turn into cooked crust. Bake at 325 degrees for 1 hour and 10 minutes or until knife comes out clean. For the topping, spread fudge over the filling. Then combine sour cream, powdered sugar and vanilla. Swirl on top of fudge topping. Return to oven and bake 5 minutes. Chill overnight. Garnish with fresh pear slices.

The pears are hidden inside.

Yield: 16 servings

Open a Backyard Bird Café! It's fun and easy. To attract cardinals, chickadees, titmice, finches, woodpeckers, nuthatches and grosbeaks, set out sunflower seeds. Sparrows, doves, juncos and towhees like white proso millet. Thistle seed attracts goldfinches and pine siskins. For blackbirds and doves, provide cracked corn, and if it's woodpeckers you want to see, try suet.

Fudgey Pecan Cake

Cake

1	cup margarine, melted	½	cup flour
1½	cups sugar	3	tablespoons water
1½	teaspoons vanilla	¾	cup pecans
3	large eggs, separated	⅛	teaspoon cream of tartar
⅔	cup unsweetened cocoa	⅛	teaspoon salt

Chocolate Glaze

2	tablespoons margarine	2	tablespoons water
2	tablespoons unsweetened cocoa	⅛	teaspoon vanilla
		1	cup confectioners' sugar

Traditionally, sassafras roots were boiled for tea — and even a beer concocted from the roots, hence the name root beer! Sassafras tea has been used as a spring tonic and as a beverage for ages. The dried, ground leaves can be used to thicken soups and gumbos.

Line bottom of a 9 inch spring form pan with foil. Butter foil and sides of pan. Heat oven to 350 degrees. In a large mixing bowl, combine margarine, sugar and vanilla. Beat well. Separate eggs. Add yolks one at a time, beating well after each addition. Blend in cocoa, flour and water. Beat well. Stir in pecans. In a small bowl, beat egg whites, cream of tartar and salt until stiff peaks form. Carefully fold into chocolate mixture. Pour into prepared pan. Bake 45 minutes or until top of cake cracks slightly. (Cake will not test done) Cool 1 hour. Chill until firm. Remove sides of pan. Prepare glaze by melting margarine in a small pan over low heat. Add cocoa and water. Stir until thickened. Do not boil. Remove from heat. Add vanilla and confectioners' sugar. Whisk to blend. Pour glaze over cake, allowing glaze to run down sides of cake. With spatula, spread glaze evenly on top and sides. Garnish with pecan halves.

Yield: 8 servings

Grandmother Wilson's Jam Cake

1	cup butter	2	teaspoons allspice
2	cups sugar	2	teaspoons cinnamon
6	eggs, beaten	2	teaspoons cloves
1	cup buttermilk	2	cups seedless blackberry jam
4	cups flour	1	cup raisins
1	tablespoon soda	1	cup chopped nuts

Cream butter and sugar; add beaten eggs and all other ingredients. Mix well. Pour batter into two greased and floured 10 inch tube or Bundt pans. Bake at 350 degrees for approximately 55 minutes.

Great with morning coffee or afternoon tea!

Yield: 24 servings

Whole cloves add a fruity taste to ham, pork and pickled fruit. Use ground cloves in baked goods and sauces. Not all cloves are used in cooking; half of the world's production is used to flavor cigarettes in Indonesia.

Chocolate Fudge Cake

Cake

1	stick margarine	1	cup self-rising flour
1	cup sugar	1	(16 ounce) can chocolate syrup
4	eggs		

Frosting

½	stick margarine	½	cup chopped pecans (can use more)
½	cup semisweet chocolate chips	⅓	cup milk
¾	cup sugar		

Cream margarine and sugar. Add eggs, one at a time, mixing until blended after each addition. Add flour and chocolate syrup, beat until blended. Bake in greased and floured Bundt pan at 350 degrees for 35 minutes. Cool. Mix all frosting ingredients and boil exactly 2 minutes. Cool slightly. Frost cake. Frosting will run off cake, just keep putting it back.

Another very easy and delicious cake!

Yield: 20 servings

Rita's Sour Cream Coffee Cake

Cake

2	sticks butter	1	teaspoon vanilla
2	cups sugar	2	cups flour
2	large eggs	¼	teaspoon salt
1	cup sour cream	1	teaspoon baking powder

Filling

2	tablespoons powdered sugar	1	tablespoon cinnamon
		½	cup chopped nuts

According to legend, a circle of mushrooms marks the spot on which fairies dance at night. If you dance inside this ring, good luck is said to follow you.

Preheat oven to 350 degrees. Generously grease and flour Bundt pan. Cream butter and sugar. Add eggs and beat well. Add sour cream and vanilla. Fold in dry ingredients. Pour ⅓ of the batter into Bundt pan. Mix filling ingredients and sprinkle ½ over batter; add another ⅓ of the batter and sprinkle with the rest of the nut mixture. Cover with remaining batter. Bake approximately 1 hour or until wooden pick inserted in center comes out clean. When cool, sprinkle with powdered sugar. Cake may be frozen and re-heated.

This cake receives artists' raves when served to them at our Continental Breakfast during Celebrate the Arts!

Yield: 12 servings

Fig Preserve Cake

Cake

1½	cups sugar	1	cup vegetable oil
2	cups all-purpose flour	3	eggs, beaten
1	teaspoon baking soda	1	cup buttermilk
1	teaspoon ground cinnamon	1	tablespoon vanilla
½	teaspoon ground allspice	1	cup Callaway Gardens Fig Preserves®
½	teaspoon ground cloves	½	cup pecans, chopped

Buttermilk Glaze

¼	cup buttermilk	1½	teaspoons cornstarch
½	cup sugar	¼	cup margarine
¼	teaspoon baking soda	1½	teaspoons vanilla

Using a large bowl, combine all dry ingredients. Mix together by hand with spoon. Form a "well" in the center. Mix all liquids together. Reserve preserves and pecans for later. Pour the liquid mixture into the "well" of dry ingredients. Blend together by hand. Add preserves and pecans. Mix well. Bake at 350 degrees for 75 minutes in oiled 10 inch Bundt pan. Cool 10 minutes before glazing. Mix all glaze ingredients together except vanilla, and bring to a boil, stirring constantly. Remove from heat. Cool. Stir in vanilla. Drizzle over cake.

Yield: 16 servings

Many of the food crops we enjoy today like peppers, beans, squash, tomatoes, potatoes, corn, chocolate and peanuts were domesticated by Mayans and Aztecs.

Best Yet Pound Cake

3	sticks butter	6	eggs
1	(8 ounce) package cream cheese	3	cups cake flour
3	cups sugar	1	tablespoon butternut flavoring

Cream butter and cream cheese together. Add sugar and continue beating. Add eggs, one at a time, beat well after each addition. Add flour gradually, mixing well. Add flavoring. Put batter in greased 10 inch tube pan. Place in a cold oven. Set temperature at 300 degrees. Bake for 1 hour 35 minutes.

Secret to success — Remove all ingredients from refrigerator 2 hours before preparing.

Use any flavoring that appeals to you.

Yield: 16 servings

Cason Callaway promoted the use of kudzu to control soil erosion and as cattle food. In fact, he planted 500 acres of kudzu at East Farm, the remnants of which still remain.

Buttermilk Pound Cake

1	stick butter	¼	teaspoon soda
1	stick margarine	1	pinch salt
3	cups sugar	1	cup buttermilk
4	large eggs	1	teaspoon vanilla
3	cups flour		

Cream butter, margarine and sugar well. Add eggs, one at a time, creaming well after each. Stir soda and salt into the flour. Add flour and milk alternately to the egg mixture, beginning and ending with flour. Add flavoring. Pour batter into a large tube pan, which has NOT been greased, but has been sprayed with cooking spray. Place cake on middle rack in cold oven. Turn temperature to 350 degrees. Set timer for one hour. DO NOT OPEN OVEN DOOR DURING THIS TIME. At the end of an hour, insert tester (or toothpick) to see if cake is done. (Ovens do vary. Do not overcook. A true oven should need 10 to 15 more minutes). When cake is done, remove from oven, and let cake cool in pan on rack on counter. Remove cake from pan.

The texture of this cake is improved by having all ingredients at room temperature.

This is an old New Orleans recipe.

Yield: 16 servings

Brown Sugar Pound Cake

Cake

1	cup vegetable shortening	3	cups all-purpose flour
1	stick margarine	½	teaspoon baking powder
1	box brown sugar (light or dark)	1	cup milk
1	cup granulated sugar	1	teaspoon vanilla flavoring
5	eggs	1	teaspoon maple flavoring
		1	cup ground nuts (optional)

Icing

1	stick margarine	1	cup brown sugar
1	cup milk	¾	cup confectioners' sugar

Cream shortening, margarine and sugars. Add eggs one at a time, beating well after each addition. Sift together dry ingredients and add alternately with milk, mixing well after each addition. Stir in flavorings. Add nuts, if desired. Bake in greased 10 inch tube pan at 325 degrees for 1 hour 25 minutes. Let cool before removing from pan (1 to 1½ hours). To prepare icing, mix margarine, milk and brown sugar. Bring to a boil, stirring to dissolve sugar. Remove from heat. Stir in confectioners' sugar until dissolved. Pour over cake.

Cake is delicious without icing.

Yield: 16 servings

The peach was first domesticated in China around 2000 BC. They were first introduced to Georgia by the Spanish around 1575 for brandy and animal food.

Century Pound Cake

1	pound butter, softened	1	teaspoon almond extract
3	cups sugar	2	teaspoons pure vanilla
6	eggs		extract
4	cups all-purpose flour		Lemon curd
¾	cup milk		

Natural music is common at Callaway Gardens. High in the treetops hundreds of male cicadas call to attract females. These male insects have special membranes that can vibrate 500 times per second to create their characteristic, rhythmic droning.

Cream butter, gradually add sugar. Beat well. Add eggs one at a time, beating well after each addition. Add flour to creamed mixture, alternately with milk, beginning and ending with flour. Mix just until blended. Stir in flavorings. Pour into greased and floured 10 inch tube pan. Bake at 300 degrees for 1 hour and 30 minutes or until toothpick inserted in center comes out clean. If not done, cook for 10 more minutes. Cool 10 minutes. Remove from pan and let cool on rack.

Serve with homemade lemon curd (or purchased lemon curd)!

Contributor's grandmother made this cake every year on her granddaughter's birthday!

Yield: 12 servings

Coconut Cream Cheese Pound Cake

½	cup butter	¼	teaspoon baking soda
½	cup vegetable shortening	¼	teaspoon salt
2	(8 ounce) packages cream cheese, softened	1	(6 ounce) package frozen coconut (thawed)
3	cups granulated sugar	1	teaspoon vanilla
6	eggs, at room temperature	1	teaspoon coconut flavoring
3	cups all-purpose flour		

Cream butter, shortening and cream cheese in a large bowl using high speed on mixer. Gradually add sugar. Add eggs one at a time, beating well after each addition. Combine flour, baking soda and salt in a bowl. Add to creamed mixture, stirring with a wooden spoon. Stir in coconut and flavorings. Pour into a 10 inch tube pan. Bake at 325 degrees for 1 hour 45 minutes. Cool in pan for 15 minutes. Remove from pan and cool completely on wire rack.

Yield: 16 servings

Chocolate Pound Cake

Cake

½	cup shortening	½	teaspoon baking powder
1	cup margarine, softened	½	teaspoon salt
3	cups sugar	½	cup cocoa
5	eggs	1¼	cups sweet milk
3	cups plain flour	1	teaspoon vanilla

Creamy Chocolate Glaze

2¼	cups sifted powdered sugar	4	tablespoons sweet milk
3	tablespoons cocoa		Chopped nuts (optional)
¼	cup softened margarine		

Cream shortening and margarine; gradually add sugar, beating until light and fluffy. Add eggs one at a time, beating well after each addition. Combine and sift flour, baking powder, salt and cocoa. Add to creamed mixture alternately with milk, beginning and ending with flour mixture. Stir in vanilla. Pour into greased and floured 10 inch tube pan. Bake at 350 degrees for 1 hour 15 minutes or until wooden pick inserted in center comes out clean. Cool 10 minutes before removing from pan. To prepare glaze, combine sugar and cocoa, mixing well. Add remaining ingredients, stir until smooth. Spread glaze on warm cake. Sprinkle with chopped nuts, if desired.

Yield: 12 servings

Kudzu isn't just a pesky vine — you can enjoy it for dinner! All parts of the plant are edible, and it is high in fiber and low in sodium.

Whipping Cream Pound Cake

1	cup butter	½	teaspoon salt
3	cups sugar	1	pint whipping cream
6	eggs at room temperature	2	teaspoons vanilla
3	cups cake flour		

Cream butter. Add sugar slowly. Continue to mix, adding eggs one at a time, and beating well after each addition. Add flour and salt alternately with cream, starting and ending with flour. (Add flour 4 times, cream 3 times). Add vanilla. Pour into greased and floured tube pan. Place in cold oven. Bake at 325 degrees 1 hour 15 minutes. DO NOT OPEN oven door during the first hour!

Yield: 16 servings

Pineapple Pound Cake

Cake

1 cup shortening	3 cups flour, divided
1 cup butter	1 (8¼ ounce) can crushed
3 cups sugar	pineapple, drained (reserve
10 eggs	juice)

Glaze

⅓ cup butter, melted	2 cups powdered sugar
Pineapple juice	

Cream shortening, butter and sugar. Add eggs, one at a time, creaming well after each addition. Add 1 cup flour and mix well. Add another cup flour and mix well. Add pineapple and last cup flour. Mix well. Grease a Bundt or tube pan. Pour in cake batter. Bake at 300 degrees for 1 hour 20 minutes. Glaze cake while hot. To prepare glaze, stir together butter, pineapple juice and sugar. Poke holes in cake and spread glaze over hot cake. Remove from pan when cake is cool.

Yield: 16 servings

Sour Cream Pound Cake

Cake

2 sticks butter	1 (8 ounce) carton sour
3 cups sugar	cream
6 eggs	½ teaspoon vanilla
3 cups flour	1 cup chopped pecans or
¼ teaspoon baking soda	walnuts (optional)

Glaze

⅔ cup sugar	⅓ cup orange juice

Cream butter. Add sugar. Mix well. Add eggs one at a time, beating well after each addition. Set aside. Sift flour with soda. Add to butter mixture alternately with sour cream. Mix well after each addition. Add vanilla and nuts. Mix well. Pour batter into 10 inch greased and floured tube pan. Bake at 325 degrees for 1½ hours. For glaze, combine ⅔ cups sugar with ⅓ cup orange juice. Mix to dissolve sugar. Pour over cake while it is still hot.

Yield: 16 servings

Herbs are easy to grow, useful plants whose history can be traced back to ancient Rome and Greece. Because of the aromatic oils they produce, herbs are used not only for culinary seasonings, but also for teas, medicines, insect repellents and fragrances. Depending on the herb, leaves, flowers, seeds or roots may be used. Many of the best known herbs are native to the Mediterranean, but each region of the world has its own native herbs.

Caramel Frosting

¼ cup sugar, browned and caramelized in heavy skillet or boiler
¼ cup very warm water
3 cups sugar

1 cup milk
½ cup margarine or butter
⅛ teaspoon soda
1 teaspoon vanilla

To the browned sugar in boiler, add water to make thin syrup. Stir in sugar, milk, butter and soda. Boil briskly for 10 minutes, stirring constantly. Cook to soft ball stage (about 45 minutes). Beat about 5 minutes on high speed; mixture will change in appearance. Spread while still "runny," but if it becomes hard to spread, add a very little bit of hot water. Easily covers a 3 layer yellow or white cake.

Yield: Approximately 2½ cups

Summer squash is among the first domesticated North American food plants.
In fact, the word squash is a shortened form of the Natick and Narraganset Indians' word, akutasquash.

Caramel Cake Icing

2 sticks butter (do not substitute)
2½ cups granulated sugar, divided
⅔ cup evaporated milk, undiluted

1 dash salt
1 teaspoon baking powder
1 teaspoon vanilla

In a 2 quart saucepan, melt butter on medium heat. Add 2 cups sugar. Stir with wooden spoon until well blended. Add evaporated milk and salt. Keep mixture hot on medium heat but not boiling (if it starts to boil, remove from heat). In small non-stick frying pan, on medium heat, melt ½ cup granulated sugar until translucent, (being careful not to burn). Immediately pour melted sugar into first mixture and let come to a full boil on medium heat; then begin timing for three minutes, stirring constantly. Remove from burner and add baking powder. Mix well. Add vanilla and beat with wooden spoon about seven minutes or until it loses its gloss. Spread on 3 cake layers.

This cake freezes well. Remove from freezer the day before serving.

Yield: 2½ cups

Lemon Cheese Icing

1	cup sugar	3	tablespoons butter
	Juice of 2 lemons	2	eggs
4	tablespoons cornstarch		

Mix all ingredients well in top of double boiler and cook over boiling water until thick enough to spread on cake layers. When stacking the cake, spread filling between layers and on top layer and around sides.

Yield: 2¹/₃ cups

Lemon Squares

1	cup butter (do not substitute)	4	eggs
2	cups flour	2	cups sugar
½	cup powdered sugar	4	tablespoons flour
¼	teaspoon salt	5	tablespoons fresh lemon juice

Blend first four ingredients. Press into bottom of 9x13 inch pan or casserole dish. Bake 15 minutes at 350 degrees. Do not brown. Cool 5 minutes. Beat together remaining ingredients. Pour over pastry. Bake at 350 degrees for 25 minutes. Remove from oven and sprinkle with powdered sugar. Cut into squares when cool.

Yield: 20 squares

Bourbon (or Rum) Balls

3	cups vanilla wafers, crushed	1½	tablespoons cocoa
1	cup powdered sugar	3	tablespoons light corn syrup
1	cup pecans, finely ground	3	ounces bourbon or rum

Mix wafer crumbs, sugar, pecans and cocoa together. Stir syrup and bourbon (or rum) together and combine with the dry ingredients. Shape mixture into 3 dozen small balls and roll in powdered sugar. Age in the refrigerator for a few days. Store in container with tight fitting lid.

Yield: 36 cookies

A hummingbird feeder outside your kitchen window is a sure way to enjoy these delightful and colorful winged acrobats. If you have a hummingbird feeder, remember: Fill the feeder with 1 part white sugar dissolved in 4 parts boiling water. Clean the feeder regularly (every three days in hot weather). Don't add red coloring to the sugar solution. Don't hang the feeder in the full sun — the solution will spoil more quickly.

100 Cookies

1 cup sugar	1 cup puffed-rice cereal
1 cup brown sugar, firmly packed	1 cup coconut
1 cup margarine, softened	1 cup quick oats
1 cup vegetable oil	½ teaspoon salt
1 egg	3½ cups flour
1 teaspoon vanilla	1 teaspoon baking soda
	1 teaspoon baking powder

In a large bowl, mix sugars, margarine, oil, egg and vanilla. Add cereal, coconut and oats. Mix well. Sift together salt, flour, soda and baking powder. Add to sugar mixture and mix well. Drop by teaspoonfuls onto greased cookie sheet. Bake 10 - 12 minutes at 350 degrees. Let cool slightly on cookie sheet, then remove to wire rack. Store in an airtight container.

Yield: Approximately 100 cookies

Peaches should ripen while on the tree, but pears should be harvested before they are fully ripe or they will be mealy.

Almond Brickle Chip Cookies

¾ cup butter or margarine, softened	1 teaspoon almond flavoring
½ cup brown sugar, firmly packed	2 cups all-purpose flour
½ cup granulated sugar	1 teaspoon soda
2 eggs	1 teaspoon salt
1 teaspoon vanilla	2 cups regular oatmeal
	1 cup almond brickle chips
	1 cup chopped nuts

Preheat oven to 350 degrees. In large mixing bowl, cream butter. Add sugars. Beat in eggs one at a time, mix until light and fluffy. Add flavorings. In another smaller bowl, sift flour, soda and salt together. Gradually add flour mixture to creamed mixture and mix well. Stir in oatmeal, brickle chips and nuts. Drop by teaspoon onto ungreased cookie sheet. Bake for approximately 10-12 minutes, or until golden brown.

Yield: 3 to 4 dozen cookies

Chocolate-Macadamia Nut Cookies

½ cup butter or margarine, softened
½ cup shortening
¾ cup brown sugar, firmly packed
½ cup sugar
1 large egg
1½ teaspoons vanilla extract

2 cups all-purpose flour
1 teaspoon baking soda
½ teaspoon salt
12 ounces semi-sweet chocolate morsels
7 ounces macadamia nuts, coarsely chopped

Beat butter and shortening at medium speed with an electric mixer until soft and creamy. Gradually add sugars, beating well. Add egg and vanilla; beat well. Combine flour, soda and salt. Gradually add to butter mixture, beating well. Stir in the chocolate morsels and nuts. Drop by rounded teaspoonful. Space 2 inches apart onto lightly greased baking sheets. Bake at 350 degrees for 8 to 10 minutes or until lightly browned. Cool slightly on baking sheets, remove to wire racks, and let cool completely.

Yield: 10 dozen cookies

Anise seeds are from an herb in the parsley family. Anise tastes much like licorice or fennel and is frequently used in cakes, breads and cookies. Anise is sold as seeds or extract.

Cranberry Balls

1 (12 ounce) bag fresh cranberries
2 oranges, seeded but not peeled
2 (3½ ounce) can coconut

3 cups raisins
2 cups sugar
2 (13¾ ounce) boxes graham cracker crumbs
3 cups nuts, finely chopped

Grind cranberries, oranges, coconut and raisins. Stir in sugar and graham cracker crumbs. Mix well. Form into small balls. Roll in nuts. Pack in airtight containers. Refrigerate, but serve at room temperature. These freeze well.

Delicious with coffee!

Yield: Approximately 100 balls

Date Bars

½	cup butter, melted	⅛	teaspoon salt
1	cup sugar	1	cup nuts, chopped fine
2	eggs, beaten well	1	cup dates, chopped fine
¾	cup flour		Confectioners' sugar
¼	teaspoon baking powder		

Mix together in order given. Spread in greased 9x13 inch pan. Bake at 350 degrees for 20 minutes. While warm, cut into bars and roll in confectioners' sugar.

Yield: 48 bars

Fanciful Fruit Squares

½	cup butter or margarine, softened	½	teaspoon baking soda
¾	cup sugar	½	teaspoon salt
¾	teaspoon vanilla extract	1	(8 ounce) carton whipped cream cheese
1	egg		Assorted fruits
2	cups flour		

Glaze

½	cup orange marmalade	2	tablespoons water

Cream butter in a large mixing bowl. Add sugar, beating until light and fluffy. Add vanilla and egg, mixing well. Combine flour, soda and salt. Add to creamed mixture, blending well. Dough will be very stiff. Cover a 10x14 inch cookie sheet with foil. Roll dough to ⅛ inch in rectangle to fit onto foil lined cookie sheet. Bake at 375 degrees for 10 to 12 minutes. Cool and remove from foil. Spread cream cheese over baked dough. Arrange slices of fruit over cream cheese. Glaze with mixture of marmalade and water. Chill. Cut into squares.

Yield: 10 to 12 servings

"She (Virginia Callaway) was the guiding light and inspiration for Callaway Gardens since its beginning. The spirit of Mrs. Callaway will live forever in her gardens and on her trails. We can celebrate her life daily as we continue her love of nature in these gardens."
— Hal Northrop, former president of Callaway Gardens

Fruit Cake Cookies

½	cup butter	2	teaspoons baking soda
1	cup brown sugar, packed	½	teaspoon ground cloves
4	small eggs	½	teaspoon cinnamon
3	tablespoons milk	½	teaspoon nutmeg
2	tablespoons fruit juice or whiskey	½	pound candied cherries
		½	pound candied pineapple
2½	cups flour (save ½ cup for fruit)	2½	cups white raisins
		6	cups nutmeats, chopped

Cream butter and sugar. Add eggs, one at a time, then add milk, juice and flour which has been blended with spices. Toss fruit with ½ cup flour and combine all ingredients. Drop by teaspoonful on greased cookie sheet. Bake at 275 degrees for about 35 minutes.

Yield: 8 dozen cookies

Graham Cracker Bars

Bars

2	packages graham crackers	1	large egg, well beaten
2	sticks margarine, melted	1	cup pecans, chopped
1	cup sugar	1⅓	cups shredded coconut
½	cup milk	1	cup graham cracker crumbs

Frosting

1	stick margarine, softened	½	teaspoon vanilla
2	tablespoons light cream	¼	cup chopped nuts
2	cups confectioners' sugar		

Line bottom of 9x13 inch casserole dish or pan with layer of whole crackers. Combine margarine, sugar, milk and egg. Cook, stirring constantly, until mixture comes to a boil. Remove from heat and add coconut, nuts and graham cracker crumbs. Spread mixture over crackers in casserole and top with another layer of whole crackers. To prepare frosting, combine margarine, cream and sugar. Beat until fluffy, then add vanilla and nuts. Spread over bars and refrigerate 2 hours. Cut in small tea bite sizes before serving.

Yield: 20 bars

❋ Gingerbread Men

Cookies

2	cups butter	3	tablespoons molasses
2	cups granulated sugar	12½	cups cake flour
2	cups light brown sugar	3	teaspoons ground ginger
4	eggs	3	teaspoons baking soda

Glaze

1	pound powdered sugar	1	teaspoon lemon extract
3-6	tablespoons water		

Soften butter by beating with mixer. Add sugar and brown sugar. Mix until smooth. Add eggs and molasses. Sift cake flour, ginger and baking soda together. Add sifted ingredients to butter mixture and mix until smooth. Refrigerate for at least 3 hours. Roll out dough to ¼ inch thickness. Cut with floured gingerbread man cutter. Place on greased cookie sheet and bake at 375 degrees for 10 to 20 minutes. Cool on pan for 10 minutes, then remove carefully onto cookie rack to cool. After cooled, apply glaze. To prepare glaze, sift powdered sugar. Add 3 to 6 tablespoons water (adjust for desired consistency) and lemon extract. Mix well.

These cookies fill your home with a rich aroma as they bake. Make an extra batch to take to a neighbor as a cheerful holiday "hello."

Yield: 24 large cookies

Do you know who is the most popular man at Fantasy In Lights?® Probably Santa Claus, you say? Well, not exactly. The hands-down winner is the ever-popular Gingerbread Man. This tasty tradition at Fantasy In Lights, with its sweet glaze and chocolate drop eyes, is the favorite of kids of all ages. Visitors consume more than 25,000 gingerbread men each year during the six weeks of Fantasy In Lights!

Mexican Wedding Cookies

2	cups all-purpose flour, sifted	1	cup butter
½	cup confectioners' sugar, sifted	1	cup pecans, finely chopped
		1	teaspoon vanilla
		½	teaspoon almond extract

Sift together flour and sugar. Work butter with a spoon until soft. Gradually add dry ingredients to butter. Mix until smooth. Add pecans, vanilla and almond extract. Mix well and shape into balls the size of walnuts. Place on ungreased cookie sheet. Bake at 350 degrees for 12 to 15 minutes, or until done. While still warm, roll in sifted confectioners' sugar.

Yield: 48 cookies

✿ *Mrs. Hand's Rocks*

1	cup butter	3	eggs
1	cup brown sugar	¼	cup water
3	cups flour	3	cups pecans
1	teaspoon cinnamon	3	cups raisins
1	teaspoon baking soda		

Mix butter and sugar together. Mix dry ingredients together; add eggs and water. Combine both mixtures along with nuts and raisins, mixing well. Drop 2 inches apart on well greased cookie sheets. Bake at 375 degrees 10 to 12 minutes or until browned.

Yield: 24 cookies

The Mrs. Hand referred to in the recipe "Mrs. Hand's Rocks" was Florence Hollis Hand, Virginia Hand Callaway's mother from Pelham, Georgia. Judson Larrabee Hand, Virginia Callaway's father, operated the J. L. Hand Trading Company, a mercantile company that remained in the Hand family until 1984.

Peanut Blossoms

1¾	cups self-rising flour	1	egg
½	cup sugar	2	tablespoons milk
½	cup brown sugar, packed	1	teaspoon vanilla extract
½	cup shortening	48	milk chocolate candy kisses
½	cup peanut butter		

Combine all ingredients except candy in large mixing bowl. Mix on lowest speed of mixer until soft dough forms. Shape dough into balls using a rounded teaspoonful for each. Roll balls in extra sugar and place on ungreased cookie sheet. Bake at 375 degrees for 10 to 12 minutes until golden brown. Remove from oven. Immediately top each cookie with a candy kiss, pressing down firmly so cookie cracks around edge.

Yield: 48 cookies

Peach Refrigerator Cookies

¾	cup butter	1	teaspoon salt
1½	cups dark brown sugar	¼	cup milk
1	large egg	1	cup chopped nuts
2½	cups flour	1	cup dried peaches
3	teaspoons baking powder		

Cream butter, sugar and egg. Sift dry ingredients and add to first mixture alternately with milk. Add nuts and peaches and mix well. Shape into rolls; wrap in waxed paper and place in freezer until ready to bake. Slice thin and bake in 400 degree oven for 12 to 15 minutes.

Yield: 5 dozen cookies

Seven Minute
One Dish Scratch Brownies

Brownies

½	cup margarine	¾	cup all-purpose flour
6	tablespoons cocoa	½	teaspoon baking powder
1	cup granulated sugar	¼	teaspoon salt
1	egg	½	cup chopped pecans
1	teaspoon vanilla extract		

Icing

1	tablespoon cocoa	1	tablespoon water
1	tablespoon margarine	½	cup powdered sugar

Put margarine and cocoa in a 9 inch round dish. Microwave on high 1 to 1½ minutes, until margarine melt. Stir in sugar, egg, vanilla, flour, baking powder and salt. Mix well by hand. Stir in nuts. Let rest on counter 10 minutes before cooking. Microwave on high 5½ to 6 minutes or until top is no longer wet. During cooking, brownies will puff up and puddles appear on top. Do not overbake. Cool 30 minutes. Trapped heat completes cooking on bottom of dish. Cut into squares. If desired, drizzle with Cocoa Icing. This is really fast and easy! To prepare icing, put cocoa, margarine and water in a 2 cup measuring cup. Microwave uncovered until margarine melts (20 to 30 seconds). Stir. Add powdered sugar. Mix until smooth. Put in zip lock bag, snip one corner and drizzle on top of brownies.

Yield: 16 servings

The cupola atop the Day Butterfly Center at the Gardens originally crowned Virginia Hand Callaway's childhood home. It was salvaged from the house and served as the centerpiece of a reflection garden for a few years before the Butterfly Center was built. When workers cleaned the cupola before raising it atop the Butterfly Center, they discovered that the metal hinges on the cupola were etched with a butterfly design. Maybe it was always meant to be the crowning glory of a butterfly center!

169

Pecan Sandies

1	cup shortening	1	teaspoon salt
1	cup sugar	1	teaspoon baking soda
½	cup brown sugar	1	cup pecans, chopped
1	teaspoon vanilla		Extra sugar for dipping
2	eggs		cookies
2⅓	cups all-purpose flour		

Cream shortening and sugars. Add vanilla and eggs and set aside. When measuring flour, spoon unsifted, into measuring cup. In a bowl, blend flour with salt and soda. Add blended dry ingredients to creamed mixture and mix well. Add nuts and mix well. Drop by teaspoonfuls onto greased cookie sheet. Bake at 350 degrees for 15 minutes. Dip top of cookies into sugar while still warm and let cool on cake racks.

Yield: 5 to 6 dozen cookies

"Virginia (Callaway) shared my concerns, beliefs and philosophies about conservation. Her deep commitment to creating a world of beauty and improving the quality of life has left a legacy that will enrich the lives of many in the decades to come."
— Lady Bird Johnson

Oatmeal Crispies

1	cup vegetable oil	1½	cups flour
1	cup light brown sugar	1	teaspoon salt
1	cup granulated sugar	1	teaspoon soda
2	eggs	3	cups quick cooking oats
1	teaspoon vanilla	½	cup nuts, finely chopped

Beat oil and sugars together. Add eggs and vanilla and beat well. Mix together flour, salt and soda and add to beaten mixture. Stir in oats and nuts. Mix well. Shape into rolls; wrap in wax paper and chill in refrigerator. Slice thin and bake at 350 degrees on ungreased cookie sheet for 10 to 12 minutes, or until nicely browned.

Rolls may be frozen for future baking.

Yield: 5 dozen cookies

Shortbread

2	cups butter (do not substitute)	1	cup self-rising flour
1	cup confectioners' sugar	¼	teaspoon salt
3	cups plain flour	¼	cup finely chopped almonds (optional)

Cream butter and sugar. With two knives or a pastry blender, cut in the flour and salt. Work it in lightly until the mixture resembles short-crust pastry. With flour dusted hands, mold into a ball. Do not knead as this toughens the dough. Handle as little as possible. Press into ungreased jelly-roll pan until it has evenly covered the entire pan. Prick dough with fork tines all over (dip fork tines into confectioners' sugar routinely as you prick). Sprinkle the finely chopped almonds all over the top of the dough. Bake in a preheated oven at 275 degrees for 45 minutes or until light, light brown. Remove from oven. While warm, cut into small squares. Do not remove from pan. When cool, remove and store in an airtight tin or plastic container. If cut it into squares AFTER it cools, shortbread tends to break into uneven pieces. If pie-shaped pieces are preferred, place small ½ inch thick rounds onto a baking sheet. Notch edges with the finger and thumb.

½ cup brown sugar may be substituted for ½ cup confectioners' sugar.

Yield: Approximately 120 pieces, depending on how small the shortbread is cut.

Notched pie shaped pieces are thought by the Scots to symbolize the sun's rays, from the early days of sun worship. Shortbread is served all year, but in Scotland it is served to the first guests of the New Year — "the first footing!"

Scottish Shortbread by Wee Angus

4½	cups flour	8	tablespoons sugar
4	tablespoons rice flour	1	pound butter

In a big bowl, cream together flour, rice flour, sugar and butter. Squeeze the mixture in your hands and between your fingers until you can mold a dough ball. Preheat oven to 325 degrees. Cut open a brown paper bag, lay it on a table and transfer the dough ball to the brown paper. Roll it out to ¾ inch thick. Pierce every square inch with the tines of a fork, making sure the tines go all the way through. Transfer the dough to a cookie sheet. Bake for 20 minutes. Lower heat to 275 degrees. Bake for 20 minutes. Remove from oven. Let cool. Cut into bite-size pieces.

Yield: 20 pieces

Snow Caps

2	egg whites		Dash of salt
½	teaspoon peppermint extract	¾	cup sugar
⅛	teaspoon cream of tartar	1	(6 ounce) package semi-sweet chocolate chips

Beat egg whites, peppermint extract, cream of tartar and salt until soft peaks form. Gradually add sugar, beating until stiff peaks form. Set aside about 30 pieces of chocolate for toppers. Carefully fold remaining chocolates into egg white mixture. Cover baking sheet with parchment or plain white paper. Drop cookie mixture by teaspoonfuls onto paper. Top each with a reserved chocolate piece. Bake in 325 degree oven 20 to 25 minutes. Remove cookies from paper to cooling rack while slightly warm.

Use mint flavored chocolate chips

Yield: 2½ dozen cookies

"More than anyone else I have ever met Cason Callaway communicated utter faith that a man can do anything he sets out to do, provided the goal is proper and good — always assuming that he uses his God-given brains to back God-given courage and determination. He was a most extraordinary combination of the daring visionary and the utterly practical. From the moment I met him he influenced my thinking. He fortified faith— faith in everything good, faith in work, faith in life. Yet he was very human. He liked good food, good company, the sound of laughter, the touch of hand on arm, the warmth of affection and love." — Paul Schubert, author of Cason Callaway of Blue Springs.

Old Fashioned Tea Cakes

⅔	cup vegetable oil	2	large eggs
2	teaspoons vanilla	2	cups self-rising flour, sifted
1	cup granulated sugar		

Cream oil, vanilla and sugar. Add eggs. Beat well. Blend flour into creamed mixture. Drop from teaspoon onto ungreased cookie sheet. Bake at 400 degrees for about 5 minutes until lightly browned. (Baking time depends on the size of the cookie.) Cool slightly. Remove from pan and cool on rack.

Yield: 4 dozen cookies

Tea Cakes

3	cups flour	1	cup sugar
2	teaspoons cream of tartar	1	cup shortening
1	teaspoon soda	2	eggs
½	teaspoon salt	1	teaspoon vanilla extract

Sift dry ingredients together. Cut in shortening. Add eggs and vanilla. Mix well. Drop by rounded teaspoons onto greased baking sheet. With sugar coated bottom of a drinking glass, press each cookie slightly. (Put glass in a teaspoon of oil and dip into sugar; the glass will not need more oil.) Bake at 425 degrees until edges are brown.

Yield: 60 Tea Cakes

Nutmeg is most commonly used in baking sweet foods such as cakes and cookies. It is available whole or ground. Whole nutmeg should be grated and added near the end of cooking so the flavor will not be diminished.

Apple Crisp

8-10	apples	1¼	cups butter or margarine, divided
½	cup sugar		
	Nutmeg	2¼	cups sugar
	Cinnamon	1½	cups flour
¼	cup water		

Cut up apples as for a pie. This should cover at least half the depth of a 9x13 inch pan. Sprinkle apples with sugar, nutmeg and cinnamon. Sprinkle over this the water and ¼ cup melted butter. Combine sugar, flour and softened butter and cover apples. Bake at 375 degrees for 45 minutes. Serve with Cool Whip, whipped cream or vanilla ice cream.

Yield: 15 servings

Best Bread Pudding

Pudding

1½ loaves bread (preferably 1 to 2 days old)
8 large egg yolks, beaten
1 whole egg
1 can evaporated milk
1 can sweetened condensed milk
1¼ cups sugar

1 teaspoon vanilla
1½ sticks margarine
1 cup apple butter or blueberry jam or peaches or guava paste
Raisins and pecans (optional)

Meringue Topping

½ teaspoon cream of tartar
5 egg whites

10 tablespoons sugar

Remove crust from bread; soak in water for 5 to 10 minutes. Pour into a colander and squeeze water out completely. Place bread in a large bowl or pot. Add whole egg and egg yolks, milks, sugar and vanilla. Melt margarine in a 9x13 inch baking pan and add to mixture. Mix thoroughly and pour back into same baking pan. Cut peaches or other fruits into pieces and insert the fruit, or dollops of jam, in rows the whole length of pan. Bake at 350 degrees for 1 hour. To prepare meringue, add cream of tartar to egg whites before beating. Beat egg whites and sugar until stiff. Spread meringue on top of baked pudding and bake until brown, approximately 15 to 20 minutes. Delicious!

Yield: 12 Servings

When buying blueberries, look for plump, fresh berries with a waxy blue color. Don't choose baskets leaking with juice.

Muscadine Ice

4 cups muscadine juice
1½ cups granulated sugar
1 teaspoon lemon juice

2 egg whites at room temperature

Boil together muscadine juice, granulated sugar and lemon juice. Chill. Place mixture into an ice cream freezer. As it forms together, begin to add the egg whites, which have been lightly beaten, ¼ at a time. Continue to freeze and serve.

Yield: 10 servings

My Mother's Homemade Ice Cream Recipe

2   cups whipping cream
2   (14 ounce) cans sweetened
     condensed milk

1   large bottle chocolate syrup
    Sugar to taste

Mix all ingredients and pour into a 4 or 6 quart ice cream maker. Add enough water to fill ⅔ full. Freeze according to manufacturer's instructions. Let ripen 1 hour.

Fresh fruits of your choice may be substituted for the syrup. Other substitutions could be: canned pineapple, pie fillings, coconut, cherries, peaches, etc. Of course fresh fruits are best!! Bananas and mangoes are especially delicious!!

Yield: 1 gallon

To ripen peaches, place in loosely closed brown paper bag. Store at room temperature, away from sunlight for several days. Be sure to check for ripeness daily.

Blackberry Sherbet

2   quarts blackberries or
     2 (16 ounce) packages,
     frozen
2   cups sugar, divided

1   envelope unflavored gelatin
½   cup boiling water
    Juice of 2 medium lemons

Wash berries and drain well. Mash. (If using frozen blackberries, thaw and mash) Combine with 1 cup sugar in a large mixing bowl. Set aside for 1 hour. Press berry mixture through a sieve. Set juice aside and discard pulp. Dissolve gelatin in boiling water in a large mixing bowl. Stir in blackberry juice. Add remaining sugar, lemon juice and enough water to make 5 cups of mixture. Pour mixture into freezer can of a 1 gallon hand-turned or electric freezer. Freeze according to manufacturer's instructions. Let ripen 1½ to 2 hours before serving. Scoop into dishes and serve immediately.

Yield: 3 quarts

Old Fashioned Lemon Ice Cream

| 3 | cups sugar | 2 | lemon rinds, grated |
| 6 | lemons (use juice only) | 2 | quarts half-and-half |

Combine sugar, lemon juice and grated rind. Let stand for 3 hours, stirring frequently. Slowly stir in 2 quarts of half-and-half. Freeze in ice cube trays or small molds. Absolutely delicious!

Yield: 1 gallon

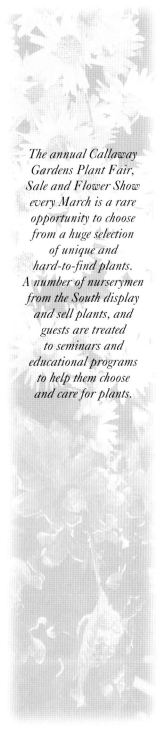

Lemon Curd

| 2 | lemons | 1 | cup sugar |
| 1 | stick butter or margarine, diced | 3 | large eggs |

Finely grate lemon rind and squeeze juice. Cook butter, sugar, lemon rind and juice in double boiler until butter melts. Beat eggs well and add small amount at a time, stirring constantly. Cook until thick. Store in jar in refrigerator. Will keep several weeks.

Makes great Christmas treats. Good on breakfast bread, Angel Food cake or over ice cream. Delicious eaten straight from the jar with a spoon!

Yield: 12 servings

Praline Cream

2	cups brown sugar (do not pack)	2	eggs
¾	cup flour	1	cup chopped pecans
1	teaspoon soda	1	(16 ounce) carton non-dairy whipped topping

Mix all the dry ingredients. Add eggs and nuts. Mix well. Pour into greased 12x13 inch pan and bake 35 to 40 minutes at 350 degrees. Cool and tear into pieces. Mix with whipped topping and freeze.

Good Winter Holiday Dessert!

Yield: 15 servings

Mary Louise's Ice Cream Dessert

4	cups crispy rice cereal	1	cup pecans
2	sticks margarine, melted	½	gallon vanilla ice cream
1	(3.5 ounce) can coconut		Chocolate syrup
1	cup light brown sugar		

Crush cereal. Add melted margarine and work in other ingredients, except ice cream and syrup. Spread on cookie sheet. Toast 3 minutes in broiler. Divide into 2 parts. Pat half of the cereal mixture into a 9x13 inch pan. Cover with softened ice cream. Swirl with chocolate syrup. Sprinkle with remaining cereal mixture. Cover with plastic wrap and store in freezer. Cut in squares to serve.

Yield: 12 servings

Blueberries may change color when cooked. Acids, such as lemon juice and vinegar, cause the blue pigment in the berries to turn into a reddish color.

Cherry Dessert

Dessert

6	egg whites	2	cups crushed saltine crackers
3	teaspoons cream of tartar	¾	cup chopped nuts
1¾	cups sugar	2	teaspoons vanilla

Topping

1	(12 ounce) carton frozen whipped topping, thawed	1	(21 ounce) can cherry pie filling

Beat egg whites until frothy. Add cream of tartar and beat until stiff. Add sugar and beat until peaks form. Fold in saltine crackers. Add nuts and vanilla. Bake in a 9x13 inch pan for 20 minutes at 350 degrees. Cool. Spread first with whipped topping, and then cherry pie filling. Refrigerate for at least 8 hours.

Yield: 15 servings

Chocolate Snappey

1 box chocolate snaps (must be snaps)
1 pint whipping cream, whipped to firm peaks
2 cups flaked coconut
1 cup chopped pecans
1 jar hot fudge sauce
Whipped topping
Mint

In a 9x5 inch loaf pan (glass is best), layer ingredients as follows: chocolate snaps, whipped cream, flaked coconut, pecans. Repeat layering until all ingredients are used, ending with whipped cream. Cover with plastic wrap and refrigerate for 24 hours. To serve, cut in squares and top with heated hot fudge sauce, whipped topping and mint sprig. This dessert is very rich.

Yield: 10 servings

Chocolate-Toffee Bar Dessert

4 egg whites
1 cup sugar
1 teaspoon vinegar
1 teaspoon vanilla
10 chilled chocolate toffee bars (2 to a packet)
1 pint heavy cream

Grease two 8 inch round cake pans and line with parchment paper. Make meringue by beating egg whites until foamy. Gradually add the sugar until egg whites are stiff. Add vinegar and vanilla. Divide into the two cake pans. Bake at 275 degrees for 1½ hours. Turn out of pans onto a rack and peel off paper. Grind toffee bars and set aside. Whip the heavy cream and fold in the ground candy, reserving about ¼ cup. Spread ½ of the cream mixture on top of one meringue. Place other meringue on top and spread remaining whipped cream mixture. Sprinkle with ¼ cup remaining candy. Chill overnight.

Heath® bars are recommended.

Yield: 8 servings

Individual Cheesecakes

1	(8 ounce) package cream cheese
3	large eggs, separated
¾	cup plus 2 tablespoons sugar, divided
	Butter to grease pans
½	box graham cracker crumbs
¾	cup sour cream
½	teaspoon vanilla
1	(21 ounce) can cherry pie filling

Beat together cream cheese, egg yolks and ¾ cup sugar in mixer until light and fluffy. Beat the egg whites and fold into cheese mixture. Butter small (bite-size) muffin pans generously. Put one tablespoon of graham cracker crumbs in each muffin cup and shake until sides and bottom are well coated. Empty out excess crumbs. Fill each cup almost full with cream cheese mixture. Bake at 350 degrees for 15 to 20 minutes. Remove from oven and cool. Fill indented places with ½ teaspoon topping made by combining sour cream, 2 tablespoons sugar and vanilla. At this point cakes may be frozen. When ready to serve, top with a cherry from the cherry pie filling.

Yield: 20 servings

Tasty Blueberry Sauce:
Crush two cups
blueberries in a
saucepan, add up
to ⅓ cup granulated
sugar to taste and
1 tablespoon fresh lemon
or lime juice.
Mix well and bring
to a boil; cook for
one minute and
add ½ teaspoon
vanilla extract.

Chocolate Chip Pizza

1½	cups sugar
½	cup dark brown sugar, packed
½	cup butter, softened
1	cup chunky peanut butter
½	teaspoon vanilla extract
1	egg
1½	cups flour
2	cups miniature marshmallows
12	ounces chocolate chips
1	cup chopped pecans

Preheat oven to 375 degrees. Combine first 7 ingredients with electric mixer. Press dough into a 12x14 inch disposable pizza pan, forming a rim around the edge. Bake for 10 minutes. Remove and sprinkle with marshmallows, chocolate chips and pecans. Bake 5 minutes more or until marshmallows are light golden. Remove from oven. Cool.

Yield: 12 to 16 pieces

Happy Peach Cobbler

4½ cups fresh peaches, sliced	1 large egg
½ fresh lemon	1 stick plus 1 tablespoon
1¼ cups sugar	butter
1 cup self-rising flour	

Use one tablespoon butter to coat a shallow 11x7 inch glass casserole dish. Slice peaches into dish. Squeeze lemon over the peaches. Mix sugar, flour and egg until fairly smooth (grainy-smooth) and crumble over top of peaches. Melt the stick of butter and gently pour over topping. Bake at 375 degrees for 30 minutes.

Great with ice cream, whipped cream or no cream!

Yield: 12 servings

The rosy blush of peaches is not indicative of ripeness, but rather is a characteristic of the variety. When checking for ripeness, make sure there is no underlying green tinge, which means the fruit was harvested before it was ripe.

Peach Mousse

1 egg white stiffly beaten	1 teaspoon vanilla
¼ cup confectioners' sugar	Peaches, chopped
1 (8 ounce) carton frozen non-dairy whipped topping	

Beat egg white. Fold in sugar, whipped topping and vanilla. Refrigerate until slightly stiff. Peel peaches, slice and beat or mash. Fold into refrigerated mixture and return to the refrigerator.

Yield: 6 servings

Creamy Banana Pudding

1	(14 ounce) can sweetened condensed milk	2	cups whipping cream, whipped
1½	cups cold water	36	vanilla wafers
1	(3½ ounce) box instant vanilla pudding mix	3	medium bananas, sliced and dipped in lemon juice

Combine condensed milk with water in large bowl. Add pudding mix, beating until well blended. Chill 5 minutes. Fold in whipped cream. Spoon 1 cup mix into large glass bowl. Top with ⅓ each vanilla wafers, bananas, pudding. Repeat layers ending with pudding. Refrigerate.

Yield: 8 to 10 servings

Quick dessert idea: Spoon blueberries into individual dishes and sprinkle with brown sugar and a dollop of sour cream or yogurt. If using oven-proof bowls, pop under the broiler for approximately three minutes or until sugar melts.

Spring Flower Angel Custard Dessert

6	eggs, separated	¼	cup cold water
1½	cups sugar, divided		Yellow food coloring
¾	cup lemon juice	2	(10 inch) store-bought angel food cakes
1½	teaspoons grated lemon rind		
1	tablespoon unflavored gelatin		

Separate eggs. Set whites aside. Combine egg yolks, ¾ cup sugar, lemon juice and rind. Cook in top of a double boiler over hot water until mixture coats a silver spoon. Remove from heat. Add gelatin, which has been softened in cold water. Cool mixture until partially set. Beat egg whites until stiff. Add ¾ cup sugar gradually, beating constantly. Fold meringue mixture into egg mixture. Tint with a few drops of yellow food coloring until a bright shade of yellow. Remove crusts from angel food cakes and tear into bite-size pieces. Put enough into tube pan to cover bottom of pan. Pour some of the custard over cake pieces. Repeat layers, ending with cake. Chill several hours before serving. Cut into wedges and top with sweetened whipped cream flavored with vanilla.

This makes a lovely Easter dessert.

Sprinkle toasted, chopped pecans and chopped cherries between layers. Unmold onto a pretty plate, frost with whipped cream and garnish with strawberries.

Yield: 12 servings

Strawberry Delight

2 cups self-rising flour	Fresh strawberries
2 sticks margarine, melted	1 cup sugar
1 cup chopped pecans	4 tablespoons flour
1 (8 ounce) package cream cheese	3 tablespoons strawberry flavor gelatin
2½ cups powdered sugar	1 cup water
1 (8 ounce) carton frozen non-diary whipped topping	

Mix self-rising flour, margarine and chopped pecans. Spread in 9x13 inch pan or casserole. Bake at 375 degrees for 20 minutes. Let cool. Mix cream cheese, powdered sugar, whipped topping and spread over cooled crust. Slice fresh strawberries and cover the second layer. Mix sugar, flour and gelatin. Add water. Cook on medium heat until clear and thick. Cool and spoon over fruit layer to make a glaze.

Any fresh fruit and accompanying flavored gelatin may be used. Peaches and blueberries are especially good!

This recipe comes to us from The Strawberry Patch in Reynolds, Georgia, where folks from all over South Georgia travel to pick their own berries.

Yield: 15 servings

*Peach equalities:
One pound of fresh peaches = 2 cups, slices*

Two pounds of fresh peaches = enough to make one 9-inch pie

One fresh medium peach = 38 calories (an excellent snack!)

Sour Cream Apple Pie

¾ cup sugar	1 cup sour cream
⅓ cup plus 2 tablespoons all-purpose flour, divided	2 cups apples, peeled and chopped
⅓ teaspoon salt	1 9 inch pie shell
1 large egg, beaten	¼ cup margarine
½ teaspoon vanilla (optional)	⅓ cup brown sugar

Combine sugar, 2 tablespoons flour and salt. Add egg, vanilla and sour cream. Add apples and pour into the pie shell. Bake at 350 degrees for 15 minutes. Reduce heat to 325 degrees. Bake 10 minutes. Remove from oven. Combine ⅓ cup flour, margarine and brown sugar, blend well. Sprinkle over pie and return to oven for 20 minutes at 325 degrees until topping is brown.

Yield: 8 servings

❋ Blueberry Pie

1	quart whole blueberries, divided	1	heaping tablespoons corn-starch
1	cup water	1	precooked pie shell
2	cups sugar		Whipping cream

Wash berries and put all but one cup in the refrigerator to chill. Cook 1 cup berries, water and sugar for 10 minutes. Remove from stove and strain through a coarse strainer. Add cornstarch, which has been dissolved in a little cold water. Cook about 20 minutes or until thick. Thoroughly chill cooked blueberries, but not until set. Place cold blueberries in a precooked 9 inch pie shell and pour chilled blueberry mixture over them. Refrigerate and serve with whipped cream.

Yield: 8 servings

One of Cason Callaway's experimental crops at his Blue Springs Farm was blueberries.

Rum Torte

1	pint whipping cream	¾	cup sugar
2	packages ladyfingers, split	4	tablespoons rum
3	eggs, separated		German chocolate, grated

Whip cream. Set aside. Line bottom of an 8x12 inch glass pan with split ladyfingers. Line sides with split ladyfingers cut in half so that the rounded end is up. Beat egg whites until stiff. Set aside. In a large bowl, beat egg yolks. Add sugar gradually, beating until creamy. Add rum, mixing thoroughly. Gently, but thoroughly, fold in whipped cream, then fold in egg whites gently, but thoroughly. Drizzle a small amount of rum over ladyfingers, careful not to saturate. Pour mixture over ladyfingers. Spread evenly. Cover and refrigerate 8 hours or overnight. Before serving, garnish with grated chocolate on top. Cut into squares to serve.

A favorite Thanksgiving and Christmas dessert.

Yield: 12 servings

Cranberry Pecan Pie

1 (12 ounce) bag fresh cranberries	½ cup pecans, roughly chopped
1 (16 ounce) can crushed pineapple, with juice	2 tablespoons flour
2 tablespoons orange juice	2 9 inch pie crusts
1½ cups sugar	1 Whipped cream, or better yet, Rum Raisin ice cream

Place cranberries, pineapple, orange juice and sugar in saucepan. Cover, cook over medium heat until sugar dissolves and cranberries start to pop. Turn off heat and stir in pecans. Allow mixture to cool. When cool, stir in flour. Preheat oven to 350 degrees. Fit one crust into a 9 inch pie pan. Spoon in filling and cover with second crust. Crimp edges. Bake pie 45 minutes or until golden. Cool and serve with ice cream or whipped cream. Easy!

Yield: 8 servings

Frozen Strawberry Pie

2 egg whites	½ pint whipping cream, whipped
1 cup sugar	1 9 inch baked pie crust
1 (10 ounce) package frozen strawberries	
1½ tablespoons fresh lemon juice	

Beat egg whites until foamy. Add sugar, strawberries and lemon juice. Beat for 15 minutes. NO LESS. Fold in whipped cream. Pour into baked pie shell. Freeze overnight or longer.

Ten ounces of fresh sliced strawberries may be used instead of frozen. If using fresh berries, a little more sugar may be needed depending on their sweetness. This recipe can be doubled easily and will yield 3 pies.

Yield: 6 servings

Grapefruit Chiffon Pie

1	tablespoon unflavored gelatin	1	tablespoon grapefruit rind, grated
¼	cup cold water	½	cup grapefruit juice with pulp
4	eggs, separated	1	tablespoon lemon juice
1	cup sugar	1	9 inch baked pie shell
	Dash salt		Whipped cream

Soften gelatin in cold water. Beat egg yolks slightly and place them and the sugar, salt, grapefruit rind, pulp and lemon juice in the upper part of a double boiler. Cook over hot water, stirring constantly, until thickened. Add gelatin and stir until dissolved. Cool. Fold in the egg whites, which have been beaten with 4 tablespoons sugar until stiff, but not dry. Turn into a baked 9 inch pie shell. Chill and serve topped with whipped cream.

A light and unusual pie!

Yield: 8 servings

Key Lime Pie

4	eggs, separated	1	9 inch graham cracker pie crust, or crust of choice
1	can sweetened condensed milk	¼	teaspoon cream of tartar
½	cup Key lime juice		Dash salt
		6	tablespoons sugar

Separate egg yolks from whites. Place whites in refrigerator until ready to make meringue. In a large bowl, add slightly beaten egg yolks to condensed milk and beat at medium speed with mixer, or by hand, until well blended. Add lime juice gradually while beating. Pour filling into pie shell. Beat egg whites with cream of tartar and salt until slight mounds form when beater is raised. Gradually add sugar until it stands in stiff peaks. Spread over pie, sealing to the edge of pastry. Bake at 325 degrees for 15 minutes or until meringue is golden brown. Let pie cool and then place in refrigerator an hour or longer before serving.

For extra high meringue, use 5 egg whites and 10 tablespoons sugar or add ½ teaspoon baking powder along with the cream of tartar. The knife, coated on both sides with butter, will cut a meringue pie cleanly.

Yield: 8 servings

Gardens' co-founder Virginia Hand Callaway was instrumental in maintaining the delicate balance of nature to the area around Callaway Gardens. She led the campaign to bring the bluebird back to Georgia and initiated a program in cooperation with the Georgia Department of Transportation to grow Georgia's native wildflowers along the state's highway and interstate system.

❋ *Muscadine Pie*

Pastry for double-crust 9 inch pie
3½ pounds muscadines, very ripe
1 tablespoon fresh lemon juice

¼ cup all-purpose flour
1-1½ cups sugar
2 tablespoons butter or margarine

Roll half of pastry to ⅛ inch thickness on a lightly floured surface; fit into a 9 inch pie plate. Set aside. Wash and mash muscadines. Separate hulls from pulp; set hulls aside. Strain pulp, reserving juice, discard seeds. Combine juice and hulls in a heavy saucepan. Cover and cook over low heat 20 to 25 minutes or until hulls are tender. Cool. Combine hull mixture, lemon juice, flour and sugar. Mix well. Pour into pastry shell. Dot with butter. Roll out remaining pastry to ⅛ inch thickness. Cut into ¾ inch wide strips, and arrange lattice fashion over filling. Trim edges. Seal and flute. Bake at 400 degrees for 10 minutes. Reduce heat to 375 degrees and bake 25 to 30 additional minutes.

Yield: 8 servings

Muscadines are the wild grapes of the South, native to the southeastern United States. The purple, one-inch fruit that ripen in late summer and early fall are one of Callaway Gardens' trademarks. Cason Callaway experimented with growing muscadines on his farm, and Virginia, his wife, used the fruit to make a tasty sauce. Today the Callaway Gardens Country Store features muscadine sauce, syrup, jam, jelly, and vinaigrette dressing.

Chocolate Almond Pie

1 (8 ounce) milk chocolate candy bar with almonds
⅓ cup milk
1½ cups miniature marshmallows

1 cup whipping cream
1 9 inch graham cracker pie crust

Break candy bar into pieces. Use a microwaveable bowl to combine chocolate, milk and marshmallows. Microwave for 1½ to 2 minutes to soften. When mixture is melted, stir until smooth. Cool completely. Whip cream until stiff. Fold into chocolate mixture. Pour into crust. Cover and chill for several hours until firm.

Yield: 6 to 8 servings

Chocolate Angel Pie

Crust

2	egg whites
⅛	teaspoon cream of tartar
⅛	teaspoon salt

½	cup sugar
½	teaspoon vanilla
½	cup chopped pecans

Filling

2	squares German sweet chocolate
3	tablespoons hot water

1	teaspoon vanilla
½	pint whipping cream, whipped

Beat egg whites until frothy. Add cream of tartar and salt. Beat until whites stand in small peaks. Add sugar gradually. Beat until very stiff. Fold in vanilla and chopped pecans. Turn into greased pie plate, shape like a piecrust in the dish. Bake at 275 degrees for 45 minutes, turn off oven and leave 15 minutes. Cool thoroughly before adding filling. To prepare filling, melt chocolate in top of double boiler, add hot water. Blend and cool. Then add vanilla and fold in whipped cream. Pour into pie shell. Refrigerate.

Best made the day before using. Really delicious!

Yield: 8 servings

Cascade chrysanthemums provide a brilliant show of color each Fall in the John A. Sibley Horticultural Center. Cascades require an extended growing season and are quite labor intensive. For this reason, they are seldom grown commercially and are usually seen at public display and botanical gardens.

Chocolate Chess Pie

½	cup margarine
½	cup cocoa
1	pinch salt
2	cups sugar
4	eggs

1	cup evaporated milk
1	cup chopped pecans
2	teaspoons vanilla
2	9 inch unbaked pie crusts

Melt margarine. Mix cocoa, salt and sugar. Beat eggs, add milk. Blend all ingredients. Pour into two 9 inch unbaked pie crusts. Bake at 350 degrees for 40 minutes.

Yield: 16 servings

Colonial Chess Pie

½	cup sugar	3	eggs
½	cup brown sugar, firmly packed	1	teaspoon vinegar
1	teaspoon flour	½	teaspoon vanilla
1	teaspoon cornmeal	¼	cup milk
1	pinch salt	¼	cup butter, melted
		1	8 inch pastry shell, unbaked

Combine the first 5 ingredients. Set aside. Mix together eggs, vinegar and vanilla. Stir dry ingredients into egg mixture. Add milk and melted butter. Beat on medium speed with an electric mixer until blended. Pour into pie shell and bake at 350 degrees for 30 minutes or until set.

Yield: 6 servings

The Dead Leaf butterfly relies on its remarkable camouflage to escape detection by birds and other predators. With its wings folded above its body, the Dead Leaf butterfly looks exactly like a dead leaf. When disturbed, the butterfly explodes into flight exposing its brilliantly colored purple and orange wings.

Lemon Chess Pie

2	cups sugar	¼	cup milk
1	tablespoon flour	2	teaspoons grated lemon rind
1	tablespoon cornmeal	¼	cup lemon juice
4	eggs, unbeaten	1	9 inch pie crust
¼	cup butter or margarine, melted		

Put sugar, flour and cornmeal in a bowl. Toss lightly with fork. Add eggs, butter, milk, lemon rind and lemon juice. Beat until smooth and thoroughly blended. Line a 9 inch pie pan with pastry (or use a deep dish frozen crust). Pour egg mixture into pie shell. Bake at 375 degrees for 35 to 45 minutes or until golden brown. Cut warm. Makes a thick 9 inch pie shimmery and golden inside.

Yield: 8 servings

Brown Sugar Pie

2   eggs
1   cup brown sugar
1   tablespoon flour

2   tablespoons butter, melted
1   tablespoon hot water
1   teaspoon vanilla

Beat eggs slightly. Add sugar, flour, butter, water and vanilla. Pour into a 9 inch pie shell. Bake at 375 degrees for about 25 minutes until set. Very rich and delicious!

Yield: 8 servings

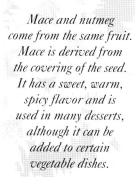

Easy Sweet Potato Pie

1½ cups sweet potatoes, cooked
     and puréed
1¼ cups sugar
½   cup butter, melted
3   eggs
1   teaspoon vanilla

½   cup evaporated milk
1   teaspoon ground nutmeg
¾   teaspoon lemon extract
1   9 inch deep dish pie shell,
     unbaked

Preheat oven to 350 degrees. In food processor bowl, combine all ingredients except the pie shell. Process until well blended. Pour into unbaked pie shell. Bake for 50 to 55 minutes or until knife inserted in center comes out clean and pie is golden brown.

Yield: 6 to 8 servings

Mace and nutmeg come from the same fruit. Mace is derived from the covering of the seed. It has a sweet, warm, spicy flavor and is used in many desserts, although it can be added to certain vegetable dishes.

Pumpkin Pie

2   eggs, slightly beaten
1¾ cups solid packed pumpkin
¾   cup sugar
½   teaspoon salt
1   teaspoon ground cinnamon

½   teaspoon ground ginger
¼   teaspoon ground cloves
1½ cups evaporated milk,
     undiluted
1   9 inch deep dish pie shell

Preheat oven to 425 degrees. Combine filling ingredients in order given. Pour into pie shell. Bake 15 minutes. Reduce temperature to 350 degrees. Bake an additional 45 minutes or until knife inserted near center comes out clean.

Yield: 8 servings

Macaroon Pie

16 soda crackers, crushed	3 egg whites
12 dates, chopped fine	¾ cup sugar
½ cup chopped pecans	½ teaspoon almond flavoring
8 maraschino cherries, chopped	

Combine crackers, dates, nuts and cherries. In another bowl, beat egg whites with sugar and almond flavoring until stiff. Fold first mixture into egg whites and turn into lightly greased pie pan. This recipe makes one large or two small pies. Bake at 350 degrees for 25 minutes. Let cool and serve with ice cream.

Yield: 12 to 16 servings

President Franklin D. Roosevelt and Cason Callaway were close friends who visited whenever Roosevelt was in Georgia receiving treatment at Warm Springs for his polio. Their relationship was so relaxed that Roosevelt often would lay aside his braces, relax and enjoy their time together as they discussed farming and other concerns of the day.

Light Peanut Butter Pie

1 (8 ounce) package lite or fat free cream cheese	1 (16 ounce) carton lite whipped topping
8 packets artificial sweetener	2 chocolate graham cracker pie shells
2 tablespoons skim milk	½ cup chopped peanuts
1 cup low fat peanut butter	

Mix cream cheese, sweetener and milk until light and fluffy. Add peanut butter and beat until smooth. Fold whipped topping into the peanut butter mixture and pour into shells. Garnish with chopped peanuts and chill 5 to 6 hours or overnight. Serve with dollop of whipped topping and drizzle of chocolate syrup, if desired.

1 cup powdered sugar may be substituted for the sweetener, but calories increase! Pie freezes well.

Yield: 12 to 16 servings

Southern Pecan Pie

3	large eggs	¼	cup butter, melted
½	cup sugar	1	cup chopped pecans
1	cup light corn syrup	1	9 inch pie crust, unbaked
1	dash salt		

Beat eggs thoroughly with sugar, syrup, salt and melted butter. Add chopped pecans, mix and pour into pie shell. Bake at 350 degrees for 35 to 40 minutes until pie is set. Cool before serving. May garnish top of pie with pecan halves before baking.

Dark corn syrup may be used in place of light if you prefer.

Cook sugar and syrup until sugar melts. Beat eggs and slowly add hot syrup, beating constantly. Add 4 tablespoons butter, 1 tablespoon vanilla and 1 cup whole pecans. Pour into unbaked pie shell and bake at 450 degrees for 10 minutes; reduce heat to 300 degrees and bake 35 minutes more.

Yield: 8 servings

Pat's Coconut Pie

4	eggs	1½	cups flaked coconut
1	stick margarine	2	tablespoons vanilla
1½	cups sugar	2	8 inch pastry shells,
⅔	cup buttermilk		unbaked

Cream eggs and margarine in large bowl. Add sugar, milk, coconut and vanilla. Mix well, then pour into 2 unbaked pie shells. Bake at 325 degrees for 1 hour. Serve warm or cold. Can be frozen.

Yield: 12 servings

In the South, as early as 1794, Thomas Jefferson was planting pecan trees. In Georgia and Alabama, settlers prized the pecan, making every effort to grow this delicious nut. Our forebears considered themselves fortunate to have land on which trees produced a good crop for personal use. For generations pecan pie has been the dessert of choice on festive occasions, and at Christmas and Thanksgiving is usually presented along with several other desserts. Pecans are served on their own, toasted, or are added to salads, rice, or whatever to enhance the dish.

Oil Pastry

2 cups flour	¼ cup cold milk
1½ teaspoons salt	½ cup salad oil

Sift flour and salt into bowl. Pour oil and cold milk into a measuring cup. DO NOT STIR. Pour into flour mixture. Stir lightly with a fork. Divide dough in halves; flatten each slightly. Roll each piece between two 12 inch squares of wax paper. Peel off top sheet of paper and fit crust, paper side up, into pie plate. Remove paper. Ready to bake if an unbaked piecrust is needed, or to fill with pie filling and bake.

Yield: 1 double or 2 single piecrusts

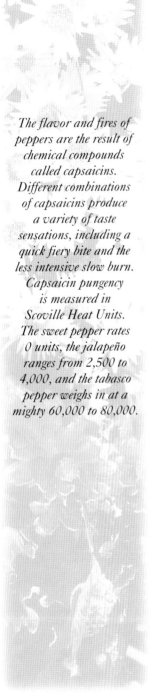

The flavor and fires of peppers are the result of chemical compounds called capsaicins. Different combinations of capsaicins produce a variety of taste sensations, including a quick fiery bite and the less intensive slow burn. Capsaicin pungency is measured in Scoville Heat Units. The sweet pepper rates 0 units, the jalapeño ranges from 2,500 to 4,000, and the tabasco pepper weighs in at a mighty 60,000 to 80,000.

Shirley Adcock
Marie Albright
Betty Joe Alger
Jane B. Allen
Michael Anderson
Anne Anthony
Lib Atkinson
Judy Banks
Ann H. Barnes
Carolyn Barr
Bill & Jessica Barrick
Melanie Bennett
Ruth Berry
Janice Boyd
Cindy Bowen
Cathy Bridges
Julia Brooks
Jean W. Brown
Penny Butler
Fran Cadenhead
Callaway Gardens
Virginia Hand Callaway
Mrs. Cason J. Callaway, Jr.
Howard H. Callaway
Peggy Campbell
Carol Cannon
Charla Cannon
Joan Cargill
Annie Kate Chambless
Lillian Champion
Trece Chancellor
Dorothy Chen
Mary Collier
Minnie Cook
Irene Cooper
Anita Dowda
Reba Dowden
Sara Traylor-Drummond
Toni Durham
Roz Edmondson
Jeanette Elben
Jean Ellis
Jean Ennis
Herschel Evans
Maybeth Fagan
Carol & Sam Faulkner
Martha Fetner
Ann Fischer
Patricia Ann Folsom
Mary I. Fox
Alice Watson Fraser
Lynda Frerichs
Christina Fritzinger
Maria Fulir
Ruth Furman

Jeanne Galloway
Betty & Emory C. Gilbert
Dolores L. Goetz
Carol Hamric
Evelyn Hargett
Lucina Heath
Kay Heberling
Fran Himic
Mary Hirko
Zereda Holland
Charlie Holmes
Terry Pearson Holmes
Donna L. Hunt
Kathryn Hunt
Bernice Hudson
Mary Ann Hudson
Martha Joiner
Polly Kirk
Sue Landa
Jane D. Lanier
Jane Lawson
Lance Lawson
Betty Lester
Mary Ann Lester
Barbara B. Lewis
Catherine B. Linz
Bonnie Lott
Jo Lupold
Marie McCollum
Doris McCullohs
Lois McDonald
Amy & Ken McGreevy
Georgina McKenna
Eva Maloy
Grace Mathis
Glory Mikkelson
Anne Miller
Carlene Mills
Jeanette Moncrief
Bette Moore
Maryann J. Morgan
Ann Morgan
Becky Morgan
Marilyn Moss
Betsy Moultrie
Anne & Jim Murphy
Cathy Nell
Bill Neil
Carolyn Nesmith
Jean Nichols
Cindy Norred
Patricia Norred
J. Nick Norred
Jerry Norred
Charlotte Northrop

Jo Oubre
Betty Perkins
Louise Perry
Virginia Porter
Madge Prebish
Sara W. Prince
Sue Pritzker
Elizabeth & James Pruitt
Charlie Sue Rambin
Frances Ramsey
Sybil Richardson
Meta Rickard
Sandra Rodgers
Martha & Nelson Sawyer
Tibby Scarbrough
Mrs. M. M. Scarbrough
Annie Scott
Myra Sills
Sibyl Slagle
Frances M. Smith
Louise Smith
Eugenia Sorrells
Kathie Sosna
Ruth W. Starr
Virginia Stewart
June Stewart
Phyllis Strain
Carol Strickland
Teresa Studebaker
Tanya Sturdivant
Joyce Tilley
Linda Tanner
Don Taylor
Didi Taylor
Virginia Taunton
Peggy Terry
Pam Thompson
Elissie Tipsword
Hazel Towle
Ann Traylor
Elizabeth Traylor
Libba Traylor
Mary Nell Traylor
Peggy Vaden
Jennie Wadsworth
Betty Wallace
Sandra Webb
Judy Weckman
Jeanne White
Sheron Williams
Jamie A. Willingham
Sally O. Willingham
Charles Wilson
Martha Yates
Margaret Zollo

RECIPE	PAGE NUMBER

RECIPE	PAGE NUMBER

Easy Exchanges

Check the first three categories for cup, tablespoon or teaspoon equivalents of liquid or dry ingredients. For fluid-ounce equivalents, see the last category.

MEASURE	EQUALS
Teaspoons	
Under ⅛ teaspoon	Dash or pinch
1½ teaspoons	½ tablespoon
3 teaspoons	1 tablespoon
Tablespoons	
1 tablespoon	3 teaspoons
4 tablespoons	¼ cup
5⅓ tablespoons	⅓ cup
8 tablespoons	½ cup
10⅔ tablespoons	⅔ cup
16 tablespoons	1 cup
Cups	
¼ cup	4 tablespoons
⅓ cup	5⅓ tablespoons
½ cup	8 tablespoons
½ cup	¼ pint
⅔ cup	10⅔ tablespoons
1 cup	16 tablespoons
1 cup	½ pint
2 cups	1 pint
4 cups	1 quart
Liquid Measures	
2 tablespoons	1 fluid ounce
3 tablespoons	1 jigger
¼ cup	2 fluid ounces
½ cup	4 fluid ounces
1 cup	8 fluid ounces

Equivalents

INGREDIENT	EQUIVALENT
3 medium apples	3 cups sliced apples
3 medium bananas	2½ cups sliced, 2 cups mashed banana
1 medium lemon	2 to 3 tablespoons juice and 2 teaspoons grated rind
1 medium lime	1½ to 2 tablespoons juice
1 medium orange	⅓ cup juice and 2 tablespoons grated rind
4 medium peaches	2 cups sliced peaches
4 medium pears	2 cups sliced pears
1 quart strawberries	4 cups sliced strawberries
1 pound head cabbage	4½ cups shredded cabbage
1 pound carrots	3 cups shredded carrots
2 medium corn ears	1 cup whole kernel corn
1 large green pepper	1 cup diced green pepper
1 pound head lettuce	6¼ cups torn lettuce
8 ounces raw mushrooms	1 cup sliced cooked mushrooms
1 medium onion	½ cup chopped onion
3 medium white potatoes	2 cups cubed cooked or 1¾ cups mashed white potatoes
3 medium sweet potatoes	3 cups sliced sweet potatoes
8 slices cooked bacon	½ cup crumbled bacon
1 pound American or Cheddar cheese	4 to 5 cups shredded cheese
4 ounces cheese	1 cup shredded cheese
5 large whole eggs	1 cup eggs
6 to 7 large eggs	1 cup egg whites
11 to 12 large eggs	1 cup egg yolks
1 cup quick-cooking oats	1¾ cups cooked oats
1 cup uncooked long grain rice	3 to 4 cups cooked rice
1 cup pre-cooked rice	2 cups cooked rice
1 pound coffee	40 cups perked coffee
1 pound pitted dates	2 to 3 cups chopped dates
1 pound all-purpose flour	4 cups flour
1 pound granulated sugar	2 cups sugar
1 pound powdered sugar	3½ cups powdered sugar
1 pound brown sugar	2¼ cups firmly packed brown sugar
1 cup (4 ounces) uncooked macaroni	2¼ cups cooked macaroni
4 ounces uncooked noodles	2 cups cooked noodles
7 ounces uncooked spaghetti	4 cups cooked spaghetti
1 pound shelled nuts	4 cups chopped nuts
1 cup whipping cream	2 cups whipped cream
1 cup soft bread crumbs	2 slices fresh bread
1 pound crab in shell	¼ to 1 cup flaked crab
1½ pounds fresh, unpeeled shrimp	2 cups cooked, peeled, deveined shrimp
1 pound fresh small shrimp	35 or more shrimp
1 pound fresh medium shrimp	26 to 35 shrimp
1 pound fresh large shrimp	21 to 25 shrimp
1 pound fresh jumbo shrimp	less than 20 shrimp
Crackers	
19 chocolate wafers	1 cup crumbs
14 graham cracker squares	1 cup fine crumbs
28 saltines	1 cup finely crushed crumbs
22 vanilla wafers	1 cup finely crushed crumbs

Ingredient Substitutions

INSTEAD OF:	AMOUNT:	USE:
Arrowroot	1 teaspoon 2 teaspoons	1 tablespoon flour 1 tablespoon cornstarch
Bacon bits	1 tablespoon	1 slice bacon
Baking powder	1 teaspoon	¼ teaspoon baking soda + ½ teaspoon cream of tartar + ¼ teaspoon cornstarch

Baking powder,
  double-acting
	1 teaspoon	1½ teaspoons phosphate
		  baking powder or 2 teaspoons
		  tartrate baking powder

Bay leaf, ground	⅛ teaspoon	1 whole bay leaf
Bay leaf, crumbled	¼ teaspoon	1 whole bay leaf
Beef soup base	1½ teaspoons 1 tablespoon + 1 cup water 1 teaspoon	1 bouillon cube 1 cup beef stock 1 teaspoon beef extract

Butter	1 cup	1 cup margarine or
		  1 cup shortening +
		  butter flavoring, or
		  ⅘ cup bacon drippings +
		  ¼ cup liquid, or
		  ⅞ cup vegetable oil

Buttermilk	1 cup	1 cup yogurt, or
		  1 cup warm milk +
		  1 tablespoon white vinegar
		  or lemon juice; allow to
		  stand for 10 minutes

Cake flour	1 cup	1 cup less 2 tablespoons
		  white flour + 2 tablespoons
		  cornstarch

Cardamom, ground	½ teaspoon	10 whole pods (pod removed, seeds crushed)

Ingredient Substitutions (continued)

INSTEAD OF:	AMOUNT:	USE:
Chicken soup base	1½ teaspoons	1 chicken bouillon cube
	1 tablespoon + 1 cup water	1 cup chicken stock
Chocolate, unsweetened	1 square	3 tablespoons cocoa + 2 teaspoons shortening
Chocolate, semisweet	1 square	3 tablespoons cocoa + 2 teaspoons shortening + 3 tablespoons sugar
Cornstarch	1 tablespoon	2 tablespoons white flour or 1 tablespoon arrowroot, or 1 tablespoon tapioca
Cracker crumbs	¾ cup	1 cup dry bread crumbs
Cream	1 cup	¾ cup milk plus ⅓ cup melted butter
Egg	1 egg	2 yolks for thickening
Flour, white	1 cup	1⅛ cups cake flour, or 1⅛ cups whole wheat flour, or 1⅓ cups rye flour
Garlic, minced	1 teaspoon	1 clove fresh garlic
Garlic powder	½ teaspoon	1 clove fresh garlic
Ginger, fresh chopped	1 teaspoon	2 teaspoons crystallized ginger (rinse off sugar coating) or ¼ teaspoon ground ginger
Herbs, dried	1 teaspoon	1 tablespoon fresh herb
Honey	1 cup	1 cup corn syrup, or 1¼ cups sugar + ¼ cup water
Horseradish, prepared	2 tablespoons	1 tablespoon dry horseradish + 1 tablespoon water
Lemon peel, dried	1 teaspoon	1 teaspoon fresh grated peel, or grated peel of 1 medium lemon, or ½ teaspoon lemon extract

Calorie Chart

Calorie Value of Various Foods is as Follows:

FOOD	AMOUNT	CALORIES
Whole milk	½ pt.	165
Skim milk	½ pt.	90
Buttermilk	½ pt.	90
Cream, coffee	1 Tbsp.	30
Egg	1 (no fat in preparation)	80
Bacon	2 strips	95
Beef roast	3 oz.	340
Beef, corned	3 oz.	180
Hamburger	3 oz.	245
Steak	3 oz.	375
Cheese, cheddar	3 oz.	345
Cheese, cottage (from skim milk)	3 oz.	75
Chicken, broiled	3 oz.	115
Lamb chop, lean	3 oz.	130
Liver, fried	3 oz.	120
Ham, baked	3 oz.	340
Pork chops	3.5 oz.	295
Veal cutlet	3 oz.	185
Fish stick, frozen	1	40
Oysters (13–19)	1 cup	160
Salmon	3 oz.	120
Shrimp	3 oz.	110
Tuna	3 oz.	170
Asparagus	1 cup	35
Green Beans	1 cup	25
Lima Beans	1 cup	150
Beets	1 cup	70
Broccoli	1 cup	45
Cabbage	1 cup	25
Carrots	1 cup	45
Cauliflower	1 cup	30
Celery	1 stalk	5
Corn	1 cup	170
Lettuce	2 large leaves	5
Mushrooms	1 cup	30
Onions	1 cup	80
Green peas	1 cup	110
Green pepper	1 medium	15
Potato, baked	5 oz.	90
Potato, mashed with milk and butter	1 cup	230
Spinach	1 cup	45
Squash, winter	1 cup	95
Sweet potato	6 oz.	155
Tomatoes	1 cup	45
Tomato catsup	1 Tbsp.	15
Turnips	1 cup	40
Apple, raw	1 medium	70
Apple sauce, sweetened	1 cup	185
Apricots, in syrup	1 cup	200

Calorie Chart

Calorie Value of Various Foods is as Follows (continued)

FOOD	AMOUNT	CALORIES
Apricots, water pack	1 cup	80
Avocado (California)	1 cup ½ inch cubes	260
Avocado (Florida)	1 cup ½ inch cubes	160
Bananas	1 medium	100
Blackberries, raw	1 cup	80
Cantaloupe	½ melon (5 inch diameter)	40
Cherries, canned soup	1 cup	120
Cranberry sauce, sweetened	1 cup	550
Dates	1 cup	505
Figs, dried	1 large	60
Fruit cocktail, canned in syrup	1 cup	175
Grapefruit	½ medium	50
Grapefruit juice, unsweetened	1 cup	95
Grapes, raw	1 cup	70
Grape juice	1 cup	165
Lemon juice	1 cup	60
Oranges	1 large	70
Orange juice (California)	1 cup	105
Orange juice (Florida)	1 cup	90
Peaches, raw	1 medium	35
Peaches, canned in heavy syrup	1 cup	185
Peaches, water pack	1 cup	65
Pears, raw	1 medium	100
Pears, canned in heavy syrup	1 cup	175
Pineapple, raw	1 cup	75
Pineapple, crushed, syrup pack	1 cup	205
Pineapple juice, canned	1 cup	120
Plums, raw	1	30
Plums, canned in heavy syrup	1 cup	185
Prunes, uncooked	4 medium	70
Prune juice, canned	1 cup	170
Raisins, dried	1 cup	460
Strawberries, raw	1 cup	55
Strawberries, frozen	10 oz.	300
Tangerines	1 medium	40
Watermelon	4 by 8 inches	120
Biscuits, baking powder	1 2½-inch	130
Rye bread	1 slice	55
White bread, enriched	1 slice	60
Whole wheat bread	1 slice	55
Cornbread	1 2¾-inch square	105
Cornflakes	1 oz.	110
Corn grits	1 cup	120
Crackers, graham	4 small or 2 medium	55
Crackers, saltines	2	35
Macaroni, cooked	1 cup	190
Noodles (egg), cooked	1 cup	200
Oatmeal, cooked	1 cup	150
Rice, (white) cooked	1 cup	200

Calorie Chart

Calorie Value of Various Foods is as Follows (continued)

FOOD	AMOUNT	CALORIES
Rolls, enriched	1	115
Spaghetti, cooked	1 cup	155
Butter	1 Tbsp.	100
Vegetable fats	1 Tbsp.	110
Margarine	1 Tbsp.	100
Oils, salad or cooking	1 Tbsp.	125
Salad Dressings:		
Blue cheese	1 Tbsp.	90
Mayonnaise	1 Tbsp.	110
French	1 Tbsp.	60
Thousand Island	1 Tbsp.	75
Jams, Marmalades, Preserves	1 Tbsp.	55
Jellies	1 Tbsp.	50
Sugar	1 Tbsp.	50
Bouillon cubes	1 cube	2
Chili sauce	1 Tbsp.	15
Gelatin dessert, plain	1 cup	155
Sherbet	1 cup	235
Soups:		
Chicken	1 cup	75
Cream soup	1 cup	200
Noodle, rice or barley	1 cup	115
Tomato, clear	1 cup	90
Vegetable	1 cup	80
Vinegar	1 Tbsp.	2
White sauce, medium	1 cup	430
Pancakes, baked	1 4-inch diameter	60
Pies:		
Apple	⅐ of 9-inch diameter pie	330
Cherry	,, ,, ,,	340
Custard	,, ,, ,,	265
Lemon meringue	,, ,, ,,	300
Mince	,, ,, ,,	340
Pumpkin	,, ,, ,,	265
Pretzels	5 small sticks	20
Fudge, plain	1 oz.	115
Angelfood cake	2-inch section	320
Butter cake, cupcake (no icing)	1 2¾-inch diameter	130
Plain cake with icing	2-inch section	110
Fruit cake	2″ × 2″ × ½″	105
Almonds and pecans	12 nuts	98
Cashews or peanuts	12 nuts	85
Peanut Butter	1 Tbsp.	105
Coca-Cola	6 oz.	80
Ginger ale	8 oz.	75
Potato chips	12 large	115

Reference: THE YEARBOOK OF AGRICULTURE 1959, *the United States Department of Agriculture, Washington, DC*

C

G

H

I

S